SOARING INTO THE STORM

A BOOK ABOUT THOSE WHO TRIUMPH OVER ADVERSITY

"MS. ASHER'S SEEMINGLY-SIMPLE PARABLE IS LIKE A RARE ORE,
STRONG AND YET INFINITELY MALLEABLE. . ."

– Jacqueline Kennedy Onassis

$17.95 In the United States
For additional copies, see the order form at the end of the book.

Proceeds from the sale of this book are donated in part to two types of organizations: those who support families and children overcoming adversity and those who help create and maintain wildlife habitat.

Printed in the USA on Acid-Free Recycled Paper
Library of Congress Cataloging-in-Publication Data Pending
ISBN 1-887703-00-4

Soaring Into The Storm Written by Alison Asher
Cover Design, Cover Illustration & All Internal Graphics Created by Alison Asher
Copyright 1996 Alison Asher

Cover Text by Nancy Newman and Claire Russel; Printing Guidance by Billy Runnels
Photography of the Cover and Clouds, by Grice & Grice; Promotions by Case & Case

Photography of the Trumpeter Swans by Richard A. Brown, Director of the Bloedel Reserve
Duotones and the rain feather contributed by The Printery

With special thanks to the Arbor Fund for their contribution to this project
And deep appreciation for the generosity of Scott Smith,
Richard A. Brown, Billy Runnels, and Ellen Roberts

LifeSkills Press 4385 South 133rd St. Seattle, Washington 98168

For My Mother, Barbara

A welcome magician who makes fears disappear.

ABOUT THE COVER ILLUSTRATION

The cover illustration introduces a new art form created by Alison Asher
which she calls NatureScaping

THE BACKGROUND MEDIUM
Honeycomb beeswax rolled onto glass
Softly lit from behind to create a stained glass window effect
The following items are layered in the beeswax:

THE SUNRISE
Hand-painted Japanese rice-paper, hand-painted silk,
Handmade Indonesian mulberry paper, and Chang Mai sacred prayer paper
Set in layers and rolled into the beeswax.

THE GRAY SWAN
The body: The outer layer of a North American paper wasp's nest
The beak: Australian silver dollar eucalyptus leaf, Japanese tree ear mushroom
And a douglas fir seed, all encircled with a single strand from an East Indian peacock feather
The eyes: Czechoslovakian glass on copper foil encircled in feathers

THE YOUNG SWAN
The eyes: Czechoslovakian glass
The body: Feathers gathered from an abandoned trumpeter swan's nest

THE MARSH GRASS
Warp threads of woven silk, and warp threads of woven rayon
Single strands taken from the moulting feathers of the male China pheasant
Strands from the moulting feathers of the East Indian peacock

THE RIVER
Hand-creased silk pressed into the beeswax

In the original art, the backlighting slowly changes revealing, subtle images layered in the beeswax.
First, the sunrise fills the sky in deep reds and golds. Then, the afternoon gradually emerges . . .
And finally, stars appear and moonlight reflects in the water.

THE LIFESKILLS FAMILY LIBRARY SERIES
A SERIES BY ALISON ASHER

I
SOARING INTO THE STORM
Triumph Over Adversity

II
SOARING LETTERS
Inspiring letters and interviews
compiled from the *Soaring Into The Storm* research

III
FLIGHT OF THE DRAGON*
Transforming Anger

IV
FEAR OF FALLING*
Overcoming Fear

POETRY

ABANDONING NOTHING
A collection of Asher's poems ranging from solemn to humorous

Flight of the Dragon and *Fear of Falling* are scheduled for release in the fall of 1998 & 1999 respectively.

INTRODUCTION

Here is a timeless treasure for the family library – a seemingly simple jewel whose value will increase with age.

We all face personal challenges in life. Why do some people become hard-hearted following an emotional ordeal, while others seem to emerge from even greater difficulty with a deeper capacity to enjoy life?

What qualities do people who triumph over adversity have in common? How do I nurture these qualities in myself? How can I teach these life-skills to my children? These are the questions that led Alison Asher to write this book.

The author interviewed hundreds of extraordinary individuals who had triumphed over adversity. She then distilled their healing stories into a simple parable – a tale that seems to delight children and adults alike. Following the parable is a detailed reference section which incorporates the counsel and advice of the remarkable people she interviewed.

School counselors have found the tale to be a helpful tool for children who were adjusting to a difficult move, recovering from the loss of a pet, or healing from a painful parental divorce.

People who are in the emergency response professions such as police officers, firefighters, and hospital personnel have shared the book with their co-workers, and many of the families they have served. Families have been pleased to find a book that can be helpful to all family members during difficult times; and senior citizens have found the story to be a comforting gift for friends who have recently been widowed or lost a beloved pet.

Soaring Into The Storm is an insightful message of compassion and understanding that will find its way off your bookshelf many times hence. Whether you are seeking step-by-step guidance through a personal storm, or reading the tale for its inspirational message alone, we believe this unusual book will become a welcome companion for many years to come.*

* The book begins with a parable that seems to delight children and adults alike. When reading the story to children under the age of eight, however, it is best to read only one chapter each evening for three consecutive nights. If you want to discuss the story with your child, please refer to the section entitled *Using This Unusual Book.*

TABLE OF CONTENTS

TRIUMPH OVER ADVERSITY
The Reference Section

WHERE DOES THE RIVER GO?

The first glow of sunrise cast golden highlights on the river.
Swirls of mist gathered the golden light, and rose toward the sky.
Small birds flew by in swooping clouds of tiny laughter . . .
And a soft silver feather twirled in the water alone.

Slowly, silently, a sad young swan glided toward the largest swan
on the river. The old swan's head was tucked under its wing.
It was enjoying a warm feathery slumber when the small one
startled it awake asking, "Do you know where the river goes?"

"Yes... I know where the river goes..." answered the round, deep, sleepy voice. "It ends in the ocean where it also begins." The long, strong neck snuggled back into its warm feather bed. All was quiet until the small voice pierced the silence once again.

"If the river goes to the ocean, then where does the ocean go?" Young Swan's head tilted slightly as it waited for a reply.

One thick gray eyelid rolled slowly open. The silent eye looked as deep as the whirling black birthplace of all light in the night sky. A wonderful warmth seemed to pool around Young Swan's soul and lift it up from the inside. Gray Swan slowly opened the other eye then yawned and stretched, and flapped its mighty wings sending comet sprays of water across the sunrise sky. The huge wings glistened silver in the sun. Settling its feathers back into

place it began to speak: "During the day, the sky snuggles close to the earth and drinks. While she sleeps, her warm white breath drifts and curls and lazily fluffs her heavenly bed. Even now she is drinking. This morning mist rising before us comes from our own river below." The small one looked up for a moment and then asked thoughtfully, "When the river floats through the sky. . . where does it go?"

"It drifts above the earth disguised as many different clouds. Each delicate disguise winds its way through the sky and finally finds its way back to the river. Then all the rivers blend as they taste the saltwater, and all their disguises dissolve when they become one ocean."

Young Swan tried to climb into a smile, but failed. Tears found their way through the small wings, hiding its face.

"Tell me about the storm you hide behind your eyes," said the old one, kindly. The little one's voice cracked as it slowly sputtered out a few restless words, "Something . . . something . . . *terrible* has happened . . ." Silence upon silence followed, and still the young one said nothing. Finally, the large swan spoke, "Have you been holding back those tears each time they try to burst forth? Do you know what happens to tears when you choke them back down into your heart?" The only answer the little one offered was the soft crackling sound of its tiny wings pressing against its small, sad face. At last Gray Swan's voice glided through the silence, "In the mornings I enjoy watching the youngsters playing their splashing games. I remember when you used to scoot and splash along with the others. It seems it was such a short time ago when you were running on the water and laughing out-loud. Then I began to hear your angry voice squawking above the rest. Lately, I have seen you hiding in the marsh grass alone. Have you been avoiding your family and friends?"

"I DON'T HAVE ANY FRIENDS!" Young Swan's mouth quivered as it tried to choke down the tears. The old one responded even more gently than before, "Have you noticed a terrible aching in your chest as though a large storm were rumbling inside you?"

The little one nodded. "This is because you have swallowed so many tears that your heart is stretched further than it has ever been stretched before. Each time you push back the storm, it becomes stronger. It may feel as though you have controlled it for a moment, but you have only changed its form for a long time to come." Young Swan's muffled voice spoke from beneath the feathers, "What do you mean when you say I have changed the *form* of my storm?"

"Let me show you what happens when the sky holds back the rain," the old one replied with a knowing smile.

THE STORM UNFURLS

Gray Swan gently tossed the feather bundle into the air. The young one came completely unfolded, squawked, and wildly flapped its wings. A strong warm wind filled the air. The small frantic wings balanced themselves on the steadily lifting current. Being careful not to lose its balance, Young Swan slowly looked behind and found the source of the warm, steady wind. It was the mighty breath of the old one. A strange feeling jiggled inside the little one's bones. The feeling kept growing and growing, rumbling over its ribs and finally bursting through its bulging lungs...
"WE ARE FLYYYYYYYING!"

They followed the river until it flowed into a vast wild water. A salty mist rose and clung to their feathers. The water was curling and crashing in thunder slaps of power, then delightfully leaping into the sky.

Young Swan could see faint rainbows hanging in the moist air. "The sky must be thirsty today," the little one whispered to itself. "When the old one told me how the river found its way to the sky, I could not *imagine* it would be this *beautiful!*"

A large mountain loomed in the distance. Thick dark clouds blanketed its ragged peaks. With every stroke of the swan's wings the mountain grew nearer. Soon the scent of wet bark, wild moss, and warm steaming soil mingled in the air. The deep, rich smells soared through the small one's heart like the unknowable magic of a sorcerer's spell.

They tilted their wings slightly, turned, and swooped down toward the dark forest floor. A sudden cold wind lifted them toward the mountain's naked white shoulders. The trees below stretched up on tiptoes for a better view of the two distant travelers.

When they finally stopped to rest themselves, there was a crisp snow under their feet and snowflakes falling through the air. At first the snow felt soft, but it soon began collecting on their backs and weighing them down. As tired as they were, they realized they must keep moving. For the first time in its life, the young one felt terribly frightened.

The mountain moaned as glaciers grew in its folds. Ice crystals clung to the canyon walls like waterfalls caught by surprise. . . .

All at once, great slabs of ice came slicing down the rocks, sliding into the white valley far below. A scraping sound like grinding broken teeth tore at their eardrums. The small one fought back the urge to scream. Then, the air fell as quiet as a giant snow leopard stalking its prey . . .

Suddenly, hailstones sliced through their feathers like burning comets. Young Swan's piercing cries echoed through the ice river canyon. The old swan slowed a bit to offer the young one cover.

A thin strip of silver-blue light appeared between the enormous clouds ahead. The old one stretched its long neck between the clouds and tore away the shimmering ribbon of sky. The sky ripped apart. Thunder echoed through the deep canyon below.

Light roared through the opening and tumbled over them. Desperately, they drank in the beauty. Soon they were encircled by huge towers of sunlit clouds. Invisible hands seemed to bathe their bones in warmth and gently pull them toward the other side of the storm. The small one was so relieved and exhausted it nestled into a deep sleep on Gray Swan's back. The silvery-blue ribbon of sky shimmered in the old one's beak as a warm wind carried them both down the other side of the mountain.

Slowly the old one's voice seemed to seep in from somewhere far away. When Gray Swan began to speak, the ribbon of sky flew from its mouth and blended into one of Young Swan's wing feathers. The beautiful new feather smelled like the rain. It glistened in the sun like thousands of silver-blue crystals all woven into perfect rows. Every shimmering detail seemed magnified and motionless in time.

The small swan snuggled into the safety of its large companion. A strong familiar voice hummed through the feathers beneath the young one's head.

"So you see my young one, when the sky pulls the soft rain further and further into itself, it becomes harder and colder. Eventually, the rain must become a snow storm, a hail storm, or even an ice storm. The same is true of the storms in your heart. Every time you pull your tears further and further into yourself, they become harder and colder. Then angry storms buildup until they *must* burst forth without any warning at all. Soon your friends are afraid to be near you, and you find yourself hiding in the marsh grass alone . . ."

THE JOURNEY HOME

Neither one spoke for a while. Finally Gray Swan said, "Do you recall how you felt in the hail storm with the horrible icy wind?"

The small one rubbed its bruises then answered, *"Yes, I do!"*

"What would you do if you saw another hail storm coming?"

"I would protect myself!"

"Isn't that the way the others respond when they see *you* coming?"

Young Swan did not answer. It waited a long time and then asked quietly, "How can I let my storm out softly?"

"By trusting the wisdom of your heart and respecting its timing. You cannot plan *when* you will cry. But, you *can* plan ways to let the tears out when they are still hot and soft."

Pale purple clouds had filled the sky by the time Gray Swan's feet skimmed the surface of the river. The young one gently slipped off the old one's back, wiggled into the familiar water and said, "The big swans are always squawking about how strong they are. I don't want them to think I am weak."

The mighty swan gently lifted the young one's head until their eyes met, "Those who lack courage flee from their storms and brag about their swift, strong wings. Only the bravest of the brave will soar straight *into* the storm."

Pausing for a moment, it added in a near whisper, "And real courage is quiet. It feels no need to clack its beak and brag."

The hot tears returned. Young Swan choked them down. Then, taking a big gulp of courage, it tried to go straight into the storm, but the tears just froze and stuck in its throat. Its heart began beating wildly. Finally the young one whispered urgently, "Can you tell me how to do it again?"

"By making a plan so the crying can continue after it starts."

"Can we make a plan now?" Young Swan asked.

"All right . . . what will you do if the crying comes at home?"

"I will just snuggle down in my nest and let the tears come."

"What will you do if it comes when you are with your friends?"

"I think I will tell them that I just need to cry for a while."

"What will you do if it comes when you are in a crowd?" The small one hesitated. Gray Swan tilted its huge head and raised one eyelid slightly. The little one took a deep breath and said bravely, "Well, I suppose I could *find* a place where I felt safe to cry . . . *quietly.*"

The sunset was rippling in the water as the flock began swimming toward the marsh grass to sleep. Gray Swan noticed the little one avoiding the eyes of the others, and offered some words of comfort. "I know you must feel very lonely now, but you are not alone at all. Everyone has their own private storms."

"*Everyone . . .* ?" Young Swan asked in complete surprise. "Yes, *everyone.* Look around you, every swan you see on the river . . ." The young one saw many swans of varying sizes and shapes. Some were stretching their necks up proudly as they glided through the water. Others were gathered in groups squawking out raucous laughter.

It was difficult to imagine any of these peaceful creatures ever feeling sad or frightened. Young Swan suddenly realized the old one was still speaking. "Some will have their first storm when they are very young. Others will have their first storm when they are older. Some have many, and others have few, but everyone has them." The little one squinted its eyes and tried to see inside the chest of each proudly passing bird.

Gray Swan chuckled and said, "You cannot see the storms from the outside; they are carried on the *inside.*"

"If we carry our storms like actors pretending to be brave, each swallowed tear will fill our hearts like a bag of stones. The eyes of swans like these are hard and flat. They will silently shout you away, and make you feel afraid."

Cold chills rattled Young Swan's bones.

The old one continued in a more promising tone, "If we allow our tears to flow when they are hot and soft, the storms pass more easily. The eyes of souls like these are clear and deep. They will call you inside, and make you feel safe."

Young Swan looked into the eyes of the others for the first time. Each pair of eyes was different from the next and yet, somehow, the same. Soon the little one found it could see straight into the hearts of the others.

There were several huge hearts that must have been stretched by many storms, and some small welcoming ones that had not yet been stretched at all. Some hearts were so full of hard tears they looked like sacks of stones; and still there were other hearts that looked just completely broken.

Then, warm familiar eyes seemed to pool around the little one's soul – eyes that looked as deep as the whirling black birth place of all light in the night sky. A warm summer shower ruffled the river. Young Swan began crying freely. The old one cradled the small weeping bundle to its warm feathered breast. The strong, steady song of Gray Swan's heart helped the tears flow more easily. Finally, the storm passed . . . and night settled gently on the water.

The air felt soft and soothing, as though their faces were nestled in the smooth skin of silence. All was quiet except for the sound of the old one's heart-drum which seemed to keep calling, "Come in . . . Come in . . . Come further in . . ."

Young Swan snuggled into the silvery feathers and sighed. The long, slow sigh fell in rhythm with the old one's breathing. Soon, the space between their breathing blended into one breath. The space between their hearts blended into one beat, and the space between their souls began to blend as well.

Young Swan suddenly knew how the rivers must feel when their edges blend as they taste the saltwater, and all their disguises dissolve when they become one ocean.

After what seemed like a long time, and no time at all, the young one pulled its head away from the warm feather drum and felt a strange new strength inside. It felt huge, powerful, and tender at the same time, as though it could call to the stars and the stars would answer — but there was no need to say anything at all.

A golden moon scribbled liquid-light on the river. Young Swan gazed at the reflections overlapping in the water. When the little one looked up, Gray Swan was gone.

Swirls of misty drapery caressed the water, and a soft silver feather twirled in the water alone. The sky held its breath. The river rolled over in sleep. Silence seeped into the shore.

Slowly, the distant mountain changed from deep purple to lavender and then to warm honey-gold. As the first glow of sunlight reached through the clouds, the young one saw something that made its heart shiver with excitement — several of its wing feathers were glistening silver in the sun! The newly feathered wings trembled with energy, then slapped the water out of mere joy. Bright comet sprays of water flew across the sunrise sky.

Young Swan turned toward the smallest swans on the river. Its warm voice rippled the water saying, "I know where the river goes." The others stopped their splashing games and eagerly gathered around to listen. Young Swan was just about to speak when a small lonely voice came from a well-hidden place in the marsh grass asking...

"Where *does* the river go?"

I welcome the storm as my terrible guest
It thunders through my bones, washing shadows from my soul
and leaves . . . my heart cleansed
my wings new
my fears at rest

– ALISON ASHER

This page can be detached if desired.

The poem on the other side of this page is intended to serve as a healing tool for those who are weathering an emotional storm. When we are in the midst of an emotional healing — especially when an upsetting dream awakens us — it is often helpful to have a tangible reminder that the pain will ease over time. The poem is simple enough to bring comfort to even a small child and will probably be most helpful if placed where it can be viewed during the first waking hours. Some possibilities might be, just above a night light, in the bathroom, or in the kitchen (perhaps on or near the refrigerator). It is designed to fit inside an 8" x 10" frame.

You may want to fold and refold along the perforated line before removing this page from the book.

Using This Unusual Book

If you are reading this section before you have read the story of the swans, it will spoil the story for you. Please go back to the beginning of the book. *Soaring Into The Storm* is designed to be a different book for each new reader. Because the book is written without reference to gender, the main characters may change *each time* you read the tale. Now that you have finished the story for the first time, ask yourself, *Did the Gray Swan remind me of anyone? Who was Young Swan?* You may have seen yourself in one of the characters, or they may have reminded you of some significant influences in your life. For example, a clergy member who previewed the manuscript felt that Gray Swan symbolized a divine presence, while a young psychologist saw both characters as different aspects of herself.

One reader was certain the older swan represented his grandmother. This image was so clear he felt *certain* it would never change. Yet while reading the story to his daughter, the clear image of his grandmother slipped away unnoticed as *he* became the older swan.

A newly bereaved mother quietly read the tale aloud at her teenage son's grave-side. As the story unfolded she was surprised to discover herself imagining the *old* swan as her *son*, while *she* became the *younger* one. In that tender moment, she suddenly felt a renewed sense of closeness with her son. The image of him sheltering her under his wing continued to resurface throughout her healing process.

Soaring Into The Storm is designed to allow our own inner information to emerge. In order to encourage children to have their own experience of the story, be careful not to use personal pronouns when discussing the swan characters. For example, take care to say *What happened to Young Swan to make **it** so sad and angry?* This allows the child to relate the story to his own life. If you say *What happened to Young Swan to make **him** so sad and angry?* the child may lose his own experience because he envisioned the small swan as a female. Once he hears an adult refer to the young one as male, his own story may disappear — the same way a dream can vanish from your mind before you have the opportunity to retain it in your conscious memory.

This book is not designed to be read cover to cover. Keep in mind that the following sections are set up as a reference guide. You may want to utilize several sections of the book, or you may want to enjoy the story alone and not venture into the reference section at all. Feel free to refer to those sections of the book which interest you the most, and ignore the rest.

Afterword

By Dr. Joyce Brothers*

From birth until death, loss and separation from those we love causes deep pain and anxiety. How do we cope with it? Usually, by the time we are adults, we have some first-hand experience with this grim presence that casts such a cloud over our spirits.

Grief knows no specific time-table. No matter how long it lasts, or how "normal" the mourning process is, loved ones are never totally forgotten. There is always a void and there are always memories that need to be talked about and shared.

When my husband died, I was overwhelmed by a torrent of mixed feelings — loss, nostalgia, wondrous memories of very special moments and then the anguished realization that I could not reach out and touch him on the bed beside me, at the breakfast table, at a play or concert, or at any time ever again. Eventually, I learned as we all do, that while time does not heal, it helps us learn to live with the empty place in our hearts.

Losses need to be discussed, honored and respected, whether the loss involves a family pet, a friend who is moving to another community, or a friend or family member who is lost in illness or death. Until we are able to respect ourselves, even in our grief, anger, and sadness, it will be difficult to respect the pain we see in others.

Alison Asher reminds us that we are all vulnerable, that, indeed, this is part of being able to love and care for others. She reminds us that all life is precious and when we experience loss, the expression of emotion is normal, acceptable, and absolutely legitimate.

*For our readers outside the United States who may not be familiar with Dr. Joyce Brothers; she holds a Ph.D. in psychology, is a well respected columnist in newspapers and magazines, and an author of several best sellers.

Author's Note

"Birds sing after a storm, so why not we?"

–ROSE KENNEDY

There are times in each of our lives when we must journey through dark storms which seem to pummel our souls. During these times we fear we may never fully recover.

We believe we may never laugh again. We fear we may always feel desperately alone. It takes tremendous courage to journey into this kind of darkness, yet this is often where the deepest transformation takes place.

The healing process takes its course one of two ways, either with or without our permission. If we remain alert to the torrents rising within, we are likely to emerge with a deeper sense of trust in ourselves and others. If we close down and do not respond to the changing tides, we are likely to remain at least partially submerged in perpetual loneliness.

Perhaps the willingness to be awkward and vulnerable in emotional situations provides one with the greatest possible strength. This simple willingness usually takes all the courage I can muster, no matter how often I practice it. When I am successful, the thoughts which generally limit my life temporarily lose their strength. They no longer have my full attention. My attention turns to the person I am listening to, the thing I am watching, the way the wind smells, the task at hand.

When supporting each other through times of adversity, it is important to remember that the door to our emotions swings from one hinge. Closing the door on uncomfortable feelings, unfortunately causes the door to swing shut on all other feelings as well. The task of remaining open can be as difficult for the one who is doing the supporting as it can be for the one who is experiencing the suffering.

It always helps to know we are not alone.

*Rose Kennedy was challenged by multiple heartbreaks during her lifetime: a husband who was unfaithful, one son who died in military service, two sons who were murdered, one daughter who died in a plane crash, and another daughter who was tragically lobotomized without Ms. Kennedy's knowledge or consent.

Triumph Over Adversity
The Reference Section

Replenishing The Soul

"We are so much more than our bodies..."

– CHRISTOPHER REEVE

Some people triumph over extreme adversity and not only heal emotionally, but emerge from the experience with a revitalized spirit. These are the exceptional people we love to be near. They allow us to feel at ease with ourselves. They make us believe in possibilities we had never seen before. We all know of people such as these, the ones whose loving eyes are deep enough to calm our fidgeting souls.

I have spent the past few years asking these extraordinary people how they faced their most profound darkness, healed their deep emotional wounds, and became the remarkable individuals they are today. As a result of the many incredible experiences I have had on this journey, I have learned four poignant lessons that will change my life forevermore:

1. Emotional tears favorably alter our physical chemistry; and repressing these tears may actually lead to physical illnesses. Recently, the medical community has discovered what mothers have known for generations — that crying is good for us. Emotional tears (tears in response to joy, sorrow, embarrassment, frustration, or physical pain) have a different chemical composition than the type of tears the eye produces to remove foreign particles.

Emotional tears can actually remove stress-induced toxic chemicals from the body. They also signal the brain to release hormones which significantly reduce pain and increase our ability to adjust to the situation psychologically (see the *Additional Research* section for further information).

2. There is an important period of time when the body is poised for emotional release following a traumatic event. If we honor that time, the healing will be more swift and thorough. If the external circumstances (or our own foibles) lead us to deny this important timing, it may become difficult — and take a great deal more courage — to heal the emotional wound later. Ask any decorated war veteran who has recovered from post traumatic stress syndrome. He will tell you that consciously diving into overwhelming emotions *after* the war took more courage than the acts of bravery for which he was decorated *during* the war.

The window of opportunity opens almost immediately following the unwanted experience, but (for most of us) the real storm moves in about three to six months later, then comes and goes for about two to three years. If we follow nature's timing, and let the emotions take their natural course within the first two years, we may fully recover. Digging for the feelings later may feel more like chiseling an iceberg, rather than being cleansed with the original storm. Even so, chiseling away seems to be well worth the effort. Over eighty percent of interviewees stated that it wasn't until they finally released the past emotional clogs (some as much as twenty years later) that the true healing took place. People from diverse cultural and economic backgrounds spoke enthusiastically about the new sense of freedom they felt once they finally let the past emotions rumble through.

3. The body must be involved. It is important to release emotions through the body — not just to talk about them, but to actually *physically* release them. The overwhelming majority of people interviewed said once they were able to physically release the emotions associated with the original incident, the deep healing finally began. Some examples included running a long distance and weeping, fighting a mattress (not just pounding on a bed, but pushing the mattress up from underneath and wrestling it around the room), or moving the emotions during some form of therapy involving the body. In most cases *tears* seemed to produce the deepest long-term transformation. Many people said it was well worth the effort to stay with the uncomfortable feelings until the tears finally came. They noticed that the results of *one* episode of deep weeping often equaled *many* weeks of recovery when they merely talked about their feelings.

This phenomenon consistently proved true for those whose original wounding ranged from experiences as dramatic as wartime torture or childhood rape, to experiences which seemed more common such as healing from an addiction, a divorce, the death of a loved one, or recovering from the trauma of a natural disaster. Reports of this nature were similar throughout each of the fourteen countries where we conducted our interviews. People seemed to find a sustainable sense of joy and vitality once they allowed themselves to experience their past emotions *physically*. One woman said that eight years after her husband's suicide she finally realized how angry she was. After having "the tantrum of a lifetime," the spring in her step returned, the tone of her voice changed, she laughed more easily, and her friends noticed she looked younger.

4. When overcoming adversity, there are clear road signs that lead to victory or defeat. I feel a great deal of gratitude toward the many people who showed me the clear road map between these two destinations. This fourth area of exploration is the most exciting to me and the one to which the remainder of this chapter is dedicated. Several of the chapters which follow will focus on the universal qualities which distinguished those people who overcame adversity successfully from those who remained emotionally wounded. This chapter highlights the traits shared by those who not only healed emotionally and physically, but those who emerged from the experience with a revitalized spirit. Of all the qualities these people shared in common, *commitment* was the fundamental building block.

Strong convictions were evident in *each* person who had come through the darkness and emerged with a renewed lust for life. This point cannot be overemphasized. Without fail, the people with a deep commitment had a more swift and thorough recovery than those who did not. Whether they were struggling through a tremendous challenge to their bodies, their spirits, or both, the level of *outcome* consistently equaled the level of the *commitment*.

Commitment to what? Well, that seemed to vary. In some cases their unwavering focus on a particular goal seemed to carry them through. In the majority of cases, however, the underlying commitment was fueled by a strong sense of love and faith. Listen for the deep convictions underscoring the testimonies from a few remarkable people:

A doctor who lives and works with the families of the Chernobyl nuclear disaster shares his experience. — Several of these children were still in utero during the meltdown — "It is difficult here. Some of the children suffer slowly and die. Others have become so fearful of invisible poison that they are afraid to eat, drink, or sleep. Many have lost their hair not as a result of exposure to radiation, but as a result of nervous disorders caused by fear. It will break your heart every day. But, a broken heart can also be an open heart. All the families who come here become a new part of my family. All these children are just like my own children. Beyond the medical treatments I offer, perhaps my most important task is to help them learn to love and trust again. I love my work. I love to make them smile; and I will never give up on any of them."

Ramona Laird, widowed for nearly four years, carries the commitment for her students until they can carry it for themselves: "I was at loose ends when my husband died. Last year I said to myself, *Quit complaining about the world Ramona! It's time to put your money where your mouth is!* Now I volunteer in a marvelous elementary school literacy program where many of the children are learning English as a second language. I work with the kids who start with several strikes against them. They are trying to adjust to a drastic change in their lives both at home and at school, to learn to read in a brand new language, and to deal with the challenges of dyslexia all at once. So many of my kids say, *I don't think I will ever get this!* I say to them, *Oh yes you will, because I am here to help you! And I will not give up on you! Believe me!* And do you know what? I don't let them give up! Then, once they catch on, they really start believing in themselves."

Horticulturist, Junkoh Harui, reflects on the tragic "relocation" experience of Japanese Americans during World War II: "My parents could live in hell and change it into heaven. They were amazing people. They had a deep faith in God. Being Japanese, we were Buddhist of course....There is a wonderful Japanese saying I can remember my father and mother using often, *gaman shi naisai*, persevere, persevere. Not necessarily fight, but *persevere*. It's a wonderful trait. It's inner strength. If you lived in hell, you certainly would need it. And we've lived in hell. But, if you have deep faith that you will overcome this, you will."

A survivor of the Tiananmen Square massacre talks about her experience: "We were frightened. We wanted our people to be free! It was worth the risk. Many of us died. It was horrible, *just horrible*. They [the government] killed some of my dear friends. Then they punished my family for what I did. Now I must hide and not contact my family at all [for the sake of their safety] until we have a new government in my country. Even though I am fortunate to be alive, this is a difficult life. I participated in the Tiananmen Square demonstration for the sake of the people I love. That is what I focus on when I feel sad. There are many more people like me who are willing to die for freedom, so I believe we will have our freedom before very long."

Sarah, a vivacious young woman in her early thirties, overcame immense emotional and physical challenges. She healed emotionally from the horrible experience of sexual assault and physically from the devastation of cancer. "Confrontation is an important part of the commitment to healing, at least it was for me. When I finally confronted the man who assaulted me face to face, I soon became very free. It was similar with the cancer. At one point I made a clear choice to accept the illness rather than fear it, fight it, or run from it. I said, *OK, I have cancer. Now I am going to dive in and deal with it!...*"

"There were very dark times in both healing processes. There were times when I could barely find the courage to go into that darkness — especially when I was healing from the sexual assault. Sometimes I feared that horrible darkness would just *consume* me! I worked through a lot of frightening emotions [in therapy] before I felt ready to confront the man who actually assaulted me.Once I did, the steady freeing feelings just kept growing and growing inside me until I just couldn't stop smiling at all! Everyone was amazed by the deep sense of joy that came over me. That was five years ago. The freeing feeling is not as intense now as it was at first, but, I certainly am enjoying my life! I am deeply thankful for my health, and I still smile a lot."

Photojournalist, Masao Endoh, simply refused to die: "When I was reporting on the war in Bosnia, I was captured by the Serbs and taken to their secret police. They stripped off my clothes and beat me for several hours, laughing. They broke my ribs. Then they left me naked in ten below zero temperatures to die alone. I think my anger kept me alive. I really wasn't going to let them win! I was *determined* to live! I just kept moving and moving on through the snow naked and angry, holding my ribs as I went along [sometimes crawling] trying to find someone to help me. Oh, I was so angry! I shouldn't have lived through it. I really don't know how I did it. I just knew I wasn't going to let them kick my frozen body in the morning and laugh...."

George Postle had this to say after losing his wife and dearest friend of 70 years. "I have lived a long life and had a lot of losses. Some of the hardest were during the war. But this has got to be the toughest thing I have ever been through. It honestly feels like half of my own body is missing.... Even so, there is a big difference between self-pity and honest grief. I'm not just talking about grieving over a death. There are all kinds of losses we must grieve in our lives. If you are not sure which one you are going through [honest grief or self-pity] watch for the *what ifs*. When you are on a trail of *what ifs* you are headed down the destructive path of self-pity. You have to catch yourself every time you go there. Don't let your mind stray down the path of *What if I had done this instead of that? What if this happens? What if that happens?* Nothing ever turns out exactly the way you imagine it anyway. . .and all those *what ifs* are just self-pity in disguise. Self-pity will drain all the love out of your life. Deep grieving will widen your heart and deepen your soul. How do I know? I've been down both roads."

Why *do* some people drown in self-pity while others seem to triumph over adversity again and again? While there are many degrees on both ends of the scale, for the sake of clarity we will divide people into two categories: two-dimensional thinkers, and three-dimensional thinkers.

Two-dimensional thinkers recognize the physical reality alone. They believe that if they cannot perceive something with their own five senses, it does not exist. For example, even though they *know* the earth is round, because their five senses only allow them to perceive the ground beneath their feet as being *down* and the sky above their heads as being *up*, they tend to forget that the sky surrounds them in all directions. They forget about the vastness of the universe which is always embracing them. Thus, they have a difficult time remembering that they are part of a greater whole. The same perception holds true in their own communities. They forget they are part of the larger human family and often feel separate from others (including their loved ones).

Two-dimensional thinkers are at a disadvantage when it comes to imagining a better future for themselves. Since they cannot imagine how releasing painful emotions in the present might improve their prospects for the future, they tend to *get over* their difficulties rather than to *go through* the experience. Similarly, since they perceive the past as literally being in the *past,* whenever former emotional memories surface, they cannot imagine these feelings as being authentic in the present.

Three-dimensional thinkers, on the other hand, know that there is more to their world than meets the eye. They do not have to believe it. They know it. For example, if someone were to ask if you believed in rocks, you would probably say something like *I don't have to believe in rocks. Rocks are real.* Three-dimensional thinkers are able to comprehend intangible concepts with the same conviction. Their imaginations are alive with three-dimensional sensory-rich images. Thus, they can imagine a better future for themselves. They feel a strong sense of connection with others and with the greater scheme of life.

Two-dimensional thinkers demonstrate the following tendencies: They accept the parameters imposed by the members of society they deem as greater authorities. They see facts as absolute truths rather than current interpretations reached by large numbers of people. They direct conversations back to their own lives, rather than showing a sincere interest in the lives of others. They often complain about things happening *to* them rather than focusing on the things that can happen *because* of them. They base the future on the past. They tend to categorize people in negative ways, often speaking of others in terms of *them* (*them* being a certain religion, a certain political party, or a certain grouping of people. The groupings of people may be cross-cultural, such as people who are *too* something — too naive, too trusting, too wealthy, etc.). They tend to lose their vitality as they age. Their commitments may waiver during times of adversity.

Three-dimensional thinkers demonstrate the following tendencies: They enjoy stretching the parameters imposed by the members of society who are generally viewed as experts. They see facts as current trends in thinking — trends which may give way to new discoveries. They show a sincere interest in others and will often steer conversations away from their own base of knowledge in an effort to learn from their peers. They know they have a strong influence over their own lives and seldom speak in terms of what others have done *to* them. They see people as individuals and are quick to note similarities between themselves and others. They tend to maintain their vitality as they age. Their commitments usually deepen during times of adversity.

Actor Christopher Reeve is a remarkable example of a three-dimensional thinker. Just sixteen weeks into his recovery from a tragic accident which left him paralyzed from the shoulders down he said, *We are so much more than our bodies.* Then he spoke about how lucky he was to be surrounded by so much love.

Yet, there was a brief period of time immediately following the accident when Mr. Reeve did slip into two-dimensional thinking. He felt disconnected from his family and the world. He feared he would become a burden on the people he loved, and he spoke openly with his wife about cutting off his life support. His wife responded by saying, *But it's still you, and I love you. I want to share my life with you.* Then his children came in the hospital room. When he realized how much they all wanted and needed him, he made a strong commitment to living his new life to the edge of its limits and beyond. He said from that moment on he never looked back.

This is the way it works with all of us. We move in and out of two and three-dimensional perspectives many times during our lives. No human being spends 100% of his or her time on one side of the line or the other. The question is, how much time do you spend on the two-dimensional side feeling cynical, resentful, and lacking hope; and how much time do you spend on the three-dimensional side feeling cheerful, productive, and encouraged?

If you spend more time in a two-dimensional perspective, your life will seem flat and a bit lonely (even in the midst of a crowd). The more time you spend in a three-dimensional perspective, the more full your life will become regardless of what your external circumstances may be.

President Nelson Mandela is another marvelous example of a three-dimensional thinker. While reflecting on his more than twenty years as a political prisoner, he recalled many times when he feared his dream for South Africa would never become a reality. He did not allow his temporary doubts to affect his unwavering commitment to end the oppressive apartheid system, however. Rather than allowing fear to consume his consciousness, he allowed his ever deepening commitment to consume his fears. Once he was released he had this to say about his experience: *As we are liberated from our own fear, our presence automatically liberates others.... As we let our own light shine we unconsciously give other people the permission to do the same.*

So what is it that allows some people's spirit to flourish in the face of incredible adversity while others seem to shrivel in less challenging situations? The answer seems to lie just beyond the door to three-dimensional thinking. The interview process for this book revealed some clear indicators for success. Time and time again the results seemed to point in the same direction. The people who had a more cynical view of life had at least four of the following six attributes in common:

1. They did not have a personal hero (someone who gave them faith in themselves).

2. Their commitments often collapsed when they became distressed.

3. They used resentment as the mortar for the walls they built between themselves and other people in their lives.

4. They separated themselves from others, believing they were inferior or superior to specific members of their society.

5. They had unresolved and unexpressed feelings about the adversity in their lives.

6. They lacked vitality (regardless of their age).

On the other hand, the people who tended to express a more vibrant view of life had at least four of the following six qualities in common:

1. Without exception, they each had a strong personal hero (most of them had several).

2. Their commitments ran very deep.

3. They felt a strong sense of belonging within society as a whole (on a global level).

4. They looked for acceptable solutions rather than blaming and resenting others.

5. They were willing to express their painful emotions when they were healing from a devastating experience.

6. They seemed to be enthusiastic and vibrant (regardless of their physical age).

When we asked people who had overcome extreme adversity how they went about it and what they would recommend to the rest of us, their advice distilled into three main points: *Relinquish, Release, and Replenish.* 1. Relinquish your resentments. 2. Release emotional storms. 3. Replenish your soul (on a regular basis).

1. Relinquish resentment. Here are a few tips: During moments of resentment toward others, we have temporarily lost our own sense of inner strength. Underneath the anger we may fear that others have some power over our lives — and perhaps, for the moment they *do*. If you want more joy and vitality in your life, listen for your resentful thoughts (*especially* in personal relationships). When you notice the resentment brewing, stop and use it as a clue in your search for your underlying sense of powerlessness. Try asking yourself, *What is it that I am afraid of? Can this person actually adversely affect my life? What choices can I make to remedy the situation while behaving in a respectful manner toward this person?* Have fun with it! Be creative. Begin by imagining outrageous and humorous scenarios until you arrive at something that is acceptable and appropriate. Then put it into practice.

Resentments come in many forms. Some are small and subtle, while others are huge and justified. Yet even the most thoroughly justified, saintly, gold-leafed resentment will drain the joy out of your life. If you are interested in wearing more smile lines in your old age, you might try the simple trick I am using currently. I made a small sign for my kitchen that reads *Resentment Free Zone*. Every time I see it I search my heart for resentment. I am always struck by the pure predictability of the process. No matter how well it may be disguised, a clear sense of powerlessness lies at the bottom of each resentful thought.

2. Release emotional storms. Don't force the feelings out inauthentically, but once they begin to surface, *dive in*. Here is some advise from Larry Crow, a single father who lost his wife and youngest child due to complications incurred during childbirth. "The freedom is so apparent following a deep emotional release that you begin to see each new episode as a blessing in disguise. You feel the pressure building and you want to run away — but then you remember the results. You have to focus on the ground you gained the last time you let that strong current of emotion just carry you along for a while."

"You must keep telling yourself *I will get through this and it's going to be much better on the other side!* Then, instead of running away, you can turn around with conviction and dive in. Sometimes I felt the deep outrage building up, but I just couldn't open the flood gates and let it out. Now I have learned that those feelings are going to find their way out one way or another, so I might as well let them go when I have the upper hand.... If I feel the pressure building, and I know I have to be to work in two hours, I make myself think of the things that get the angry tears going. Then I let the pressure off at home, rather than having it burst out by surprise in the office.... My son and I are getting through this thing together. It's tough, but truly, we know we are going to be all right."

3. Replenish the soul. Just as the river must find its way to the ocean, each of us must find our own way to our source and replenish our souls. This is an *essential* piece in the healing process. Just as a physical wound must heal from the depths upward, an emotional wound begins healing in the depths of the spirit.

Some of us may flinch at words like *spirit* and *soul* for good reason. Many people have been deeply disappointed by religious role models whose seemingly pure words only thinly veiled their appalling behaviors. While there are *many* exemplary religious people in the world, there are also abusive individuals to be found within every country, every culture, and every religious practice around the globe. When I speak about healing the spirit, however, I am not referring to any particular religious practice. I am referring to the place that contains the well springs of your imagination — that which allows you to hope and dream.

Keep in mind that the overwhelming majority of people who triumph over adversity say they feel deeply connected with the infinite fabric of life. They may express themselves in different languages and use different terms for the life-force we all share, but they all seem to be very confident there is more to life than our limited five senses are capable of revealing to us.

When faced with overwhelming hardships, however, everyone tends to slip into periods of extreme loneliness. (If you are in the process of healing a broken heart, you know what I am talking about.) Remember that by indulging in feelings of separateness you are temporarily affecting the neurochemistry in your brain and opening the gateways to two-dimensional thinking.

Take some strength and courage from people who have traversed darker canyons than you or I and have found their way back into the light. Begin by blazing your own unique trail. If emotionally charged words stand in your way, throw out the old words and find a new way home to a peaceful place in your soul. Watch for the telltale road signs along the way. Resentment, separateness, and powerlessness are always intertwined. Where you find one, you will soon find the other two.

When I begin feeling overwhelmed and alone, I try to view life from the telescope or the microscope. I imagine the universe churning with incomprehensible power and glorious beauty or I imagine a tiny seed with its molecules pulsing in perfect order. I like to think of the enormous life-force inside the seed's shell, its perfectly constructed memory, and its remarkable ability to create multiple generations of itself.

When I asked my grandson what we should do when we feel alone, this was his advice:

Nobody has to be alone
in the night
because the angels are always there.
When you dream, they take you
into the universe.

First,
the sky smells like rain,
then it turns into lots of different
colors with stars all around forever.
. . . so nobody has to be alone
in the night at all.

Nobody has to be alone
in the day
because there are so many
best friends you haven't met yet,
just waiting to
meet you!

– SAMUEL PARKER

How Do We Support Each Other?

"When did all this happen, this rain and snow bending green branches,
this turning of light to shadow in my throat. . .
when did the loose fires inside me begin *not* to burn?"

– GRETEL EHRLICH, from *Islands, the Universe, Home*

No matter how closely someone else's experience may seem to mirror our own, presuming to know what another person is going through can be damaging to any relationship (especially within the family).

We all have very private experiences. We all live separate lives together — and, no matter how much we may want to understand the lives of our loved ones, we can never truly see what they are seeing, or feel what they are feeling. Perhaps the best way to touch one another deeply is to embrace heart to heart, while cradling separate souls.

When someone is hurting, don't make the tragic mistake of saying, *I know just how you feel.* Try saying something like, *I care about you so much, it just breaks my heart to know that you are going through this.* Keep in mind that the most challenging phase of the recovery process can come four to six months after a tragedy. This is when your support may be needed most.

Try to avoid statements like, *there will be another. . .* (baby, marriage, home, etc.). The loss they are experiencing now is very real and absolutely unique. It cannot be replaced.

Most painful errors can be avoided by simply asking ourselves one important question: *"Am I trying to fix it?"* Even the most well-meaning gesture offered from a need to *fix it* will come across as intrusive. When I find myself wanting to repair someone else's life, I try to settle into a deep sense of honor and respect before I take any action. Then the urge to fix it usually disappears fairly quickly.

The desire to fix someone else comes from our own personal fears. Regardless of our deepest good intentions, if we contribute to others from a place of fear, we contribute more fear and anger to the situation. If this blanket rule seems a bit unfeasible, just recall your response the last time someone tried to fix your life.

Although our life experiences may be unique, our overall needs in times of crisis can be sweepingly universal. Most of us need to know we are not alone. We need someone who will listen to us. We need a break from highly demanding cognitive tasks. We need a clear sense of closeness with people we love, and some quiet time for reflection.

I recently received two phone calls which reminded me about the need for closeness combined with quiet. One call was from a dear friend whose mother had just been diagnosed with a catastrophic illness; the other was from a friend whose spouse had died. In each case I asked my friends what they needed. Both of them asked me just to be with them. One of them even said, "I know this is a long distance call, but please don't say anything. I just want you to sit with me so I don't have to be alone right now."

This quiet phase of emotional healing reminds me of the tender process which takes place during a physical healing. When bone and tissue are weaving new webs across a wound, the process takes its course softly, silently. Rest is needed to allow the body to work its miracles. This is why the hospital staff requests that visitors speak softly and stay for a short period of time. An emotional healing follows the body's timing in similar ways, but seldom receives the same nurturing response in our culture.

When we are healing from a physical injury, the bruising, the stitches, or the cast can alert others to our frail condition. These visible clues may prompt nurturing responses from others. For example if a stranger hobbles into a grocery store with his leg in a cast, most people will respond with empathy and try to be as helpful as possible.

When we are injured emotionally, however, the external clues may be much more subtle. Unlike many other cultures where a grieving costume is worn for a specified period of time, the only physical sign of an emotional injury may be the broken look on a person's face. The feeling of despair can be difficult to hide and may prompt inappropriate, judgmental reactions from others — reactions which may leave us feeling even more injured and isolated.

I was grocery shopping one day when this discrepancy between support for physical healing and support for emotional healing was very clearly illustrated. I was the third person in line at the check out stand. The first in line was an athletic looking young man with a broken leg. Following him was a withdrawn woman in her late twenties. The checker and the man on crutches were engaged in boisterous laughter while exchanging tales about bad tumbles they had taken while skiing.

As the young man leaned toward the counter to write his check, one of his crutches slid away from him. The withdrawn woman caught it and handed it back to him. He was still laughing about a comment the checker had made, when he turned to the young woman to receive the fallen crutch. The look on her face must have startled him because he said, *What happened to you!?! You look like your dog just died!* The woman looked him straight in the face and said, *No, it was my son...*

Everyone froze. Then the woman hid her face in her hands and began sobbing.

I pushed my basket back to let her out of the line, but she did not notice me. She just stood there with her face in her hands trying to disappear. I put my hand on her shoulder and whispered, *Come with me.* We went to my car where she was able to weep freely. I told her about some of my own grocery store episodes when I was recovering from previous personal tragedies. We talked about how difficult it can be to go out in public when you are feeling so very vulnerable, and how insensitive others can be (unknowingly).

If we wore casts over our broken hearts perhaps others would offer the unspoken empathy which is so necessary during difficult times. The black arm-band, black veil, or white shroud serves this purpose in some cultures. The absence of an established grieving costume leaves the society lost in so many ways.

Because there is no external sign that someone in a crowd is mourning, we miss the opportunity to respond with compassion. We tend to forget that there are always those among us who are healing *emotionally* — just as the young man in the cast was healing *physically*. This creates an illusion that misfortune never strikes close to home. When tragedy does strike us personally (in a society that tends to hide its sorrow) we can end up feeling very alone. This illusion of separateness prevails wherever time-honored traditions have been lost. In culturally diverse societies such as the United States, Canada, Australia, and much of Europe (where grieving attire is seldom worn) we must constantly let others know what we need by relying entirely upon our verbal communication skills.

Unfortunately, our verbal skills diminish while we are hurting. This gives rise to many additional problems. Not only are we completely overwhelmed emotionally, we are often unable to make important decisions wisely or accomplish routine tasks effectively. When friends and family ask what they can do to help, we may not even *know* what we need. Thus, our potential support system may falter.

In many other cultures, established community traditions leave no question as to the appropriate action each individual should take in times of tragedy. This type of cultural influence allows the community to nurture the grieving family in unspoken ways which are absolutely acceptable to all concerned.

On the Indonesian island of Bali, in the village of Ubud, for example, the community assists the immediate family in a lengthy mourning process. Friends and neighbors assume the family's duties of tending their children, their rice fields, and the sale or barter of their handmade goods. Most of the immediate and extended family members focus on preparations for the cremation ceremony. By the time the ceremony has taken place, the entire community has participated in some form of preparation for the ceremony. The family has been cared for, and plans have been made to provide for the long-term needs of the widowed spouse. Rituals such as these provide the framework for the community to respond similarly to other traumatic situations, such as when a family loses its home in a fire, or a child is stricken suddenly with a serious illness.

Community support in times of tragedy is not restricted to any one religion or any particular place on the globe. It is simply more pronounced in rural environments where people are well known to each other and the tasks of the immediate family are more easily assumed by others. The number of neighbors who may be qualified to bring in the harvest or run the corner market may be much higher than the number of neighbors who are qualified to program a computer or manage a large corporation.

Often when we want to help someone else, we don't know what to do. Then, when the roles are reversed and we need help from others, we do not know how to ask. When the supporting roles of the community are not well defined, we must be bold about asking specific friends, family members and co-workers to fill those roles.

When offering support to others, take care to be very specific. *Let me know if there is anything I can do for you...* is not concrete enough for most people who are in the non-cognitive phase of their recovery. Offer to do specific things like mowing their lawn every Wednesday for the next three months, or walking their children to the school bus everyday for the next six weeks.

If the person in crisis is a close family member, you might offer to manage the bills for two months, or do the grocery shopping for three weeks. Remember, cognitive skills diminish when one is adjusting to a tragedy. Depending on the situation, something as simple as grocery shopping can become very difficult. Routine tasks such as paying the bills and balancing the checkbook can be completely overwhelming!

Be creative. If you live a great distance from the person you want to support, mail them something once a week for twelve weeks. Just a loving card with a short, simple note can brighten anyone's darkest day.

When my grandma died, I had my first experience supporting a widower through a devastating loss. My grandfather was so completely overwhelmed for the first few weeks that he even had trouble forming complete sentences. We often wept openly together and, as time passed, we began sharing some wonderful memories about the amazing woman we both dearly loved. One of the things he said he appreciated most was the series of notes I left after visiting him.

I wrote him about twenty-five small messages just before I left and hid them around his apartment — folded into his socks, under the sixth cereal bowl in the cupboard, etc. Some of the notes began with phrases like, *Remember the wonderful time we had when..., Thank you for..., I love you because...,* while others contained just a few quick words to remind him he was loved, like *Here's a good-morning-kiss,* or *Keep this note in your pocket today. There is a hug inside.*

> We
> can do
> no great deeds,
> only small ones with
> great love.
>
> – MOTHER TERESA

61

Tips for Releasing Emotions

"Do I contradict myself?
Very well then, I contradict myself. . . "

—WALT WHITMAN from, *Song of Myself*

Logic and emotion do not run in the same channels. Yet every time we become upset, the mind frantically searches for a logical explanation. Every human being goes through the same initial process of trying to fit feelings into thoughts. We do this because verbal internal organization (talking over our experiences mentally) is always the first step toward integrating emotional episodes in the mind. It is the first step, not the *only* one, and certainly not the most *rewarding* one!

I love the expression, *I can't figure it out*! When I hear this phrase the image of a frustrated accountant comes to mind. I imagine him desperately trying to add up columns of emotions, while the emotions are jumping off his ledger sheet, banging on the door, and trying with all their might just to *get out*!

Just as this mental image suggests, when we attempt to keep our emotions under control, we actually allow *them* to control *us*. They can be sly and squiggly creatures who always find their way out, one way or another, either with or without our permission. If we release them when they are new, they usually pour out in a fairly manageable manner. If we allow them time to build-up their forces, however, they can suddenly burst out without any warning and scare the bejeebers out of us!

How do we allow the emotions to move through when they are still new and malleable? If you ask several people this question you will find there are as many ways as you can imagine, and more. A few recommendations from some of my favorite interviewees follow:

- Lose yourself in an emotional novel. Let your tears and anger out for some one else's life for a while. Sometimes that's the best possible way to prime the pump.

- Fix a car. Then you can yell and throw things and the neighbors won't wonder.

- Split firewood until you can't stand up.

- Clean your closets, with vigor!

- Go for a drive. Roll up the windows… and SCREEEAM!

- I do my Bonsai. Many think making young trees look old is a peaceful practice. Not so. You must *harm* the tree then heal it each step of the way. Pain, healing, and growth with character. Does this sound familiar?

- Smash glass! The sound is incredible…very satisfying. You can use it for anger, sorrow, rage, boredom, anything. If you smash glass it will change your mood! [This interviewee smashed empty bottles for several hours after discovering that her husband was unfaithful. She said it probably saved her life — and his. If you choose to use this method, wear gloves and safety glasses.]

- Go to any sports event, anywhere, and act like an out-of-control fan. The out-of-control part is easy, just be darn sure to root for the same side you are sitting on.

- Run and run and run. It feels great and is good for you. If you cannot run *outside* get yourself a small trampoline and run *inside*.

- Close your eyes and find the place in your body where the tension is. Then allow the energy to come out though your voice. Sometimes it sounds like humming and other times it sounds like growling. Just release the tension through sound. That's what I do every day in the tub after work.

- Turn the stereo up, and then take a long shower and yell until you don't want to yell anymore. No one will even hear you.

- If the feelings hit you hard in public, pretend like you just stubbed your toe. You can jump around and yell or just huff and puff and let off some steam. That's exactly what I did in a parking lot when I saw my ex-wife with her new husband. The rage seemed like it was going to stampede right through me! I couldn't hold it back….Thank God I did stub my toe for real! I just yelled *OW-oo!*, held on to my foot, and let it loose!

- DANCE! Crank your stereo *way* up and just dance. Don't try to do a dance. Don't try to look good. Just move around until you're soaked. If you can't crank it up because it's late at night, wear headphones and dance. Just dance! Do it! It always works. *Always!*

- Bake bread. Just squeeze and beat the heck out of it. You will feel great. Your home will smell great, and your family will love you for it. I think it is the best possible way to turn hateful feelings into love.

- Create things. Anything. Do something three dimensional like building a bookshelf or working in clay. Painting is too small and gets your mind going — at least it does for me. I get too self-critical when I paint. But when you build something by hand, you can saw and hammer and really get yourself going. Don't use any power tools. When you create things by hand you can get your whole body involved.

- If you are desperately trying to find employment after graduate school (and you are as completely discouraged as I was), take my brother's advice. Close your eyes and repeat the six secret words of success . . . *"Do you want fries with that?"*

- Cook. Make a difficult recipe, but not a new one. If you are already frustrated and you try a new one that doesn't come out, you're in trouble. But if you make something good — something you can share with the people you love — it's a wonderful feeling. If you are angry and sad, make a recipe that calls for pounding on garlic cloves and cutting lots of onions.

- If it's summer, you can beat the rugs. If it's winter, you can go skiing. If it's spring, you can plant a garden. If it's fall, you can go for a long walk and let the wild wind carry your troubles away. I love the wind, especially on warm starry nights.

- Sing inspirational songs. Sing with your whole heart. There are songs about every possible feeling. You can sing anytime, anywhere. Sometimes you will have to hum quietly in crowded places, but you can always get the feelings moving in song.

- Music helps everybody. Just go home to your music and just be in it. I love music in the bathtub with candle light. I lock the door and just let the tears wash through.

- Anger is the toughest one for me. I figure no matter where I am, or what I am doing, it is better to go for a walk than to stay where I am. I already have far too many regrets. Now I walk until I calm down.

- Try pushing the emotions past their own comfort zone. If you are feeling guilty, instead of fighting it off for days at a time, see if you can keep it up intensely for an hour. I find it usually lasts about twenty minutes at best. This works for anger and sorrow too. Just try exaggerating it rather than resisting it. Let it go! Give it all you've got!

Turning The Tide

"Love from one being to another can only be that two solitudes come nearer, recognize, protect, and comfort each other."

—HAN SUYIN, Chinese writer and physician

There is a time immediately following a tragedy when most of us can remain fairly controlled — our thinking remains logical, our movements become systematic. During this initial phase of integrating the experience, we will usually talk to any available listener.

Once this phase passes an emotional catharsis follows, interspersed with times when thoughts become wordless. For most of us, these overwhelming emotional waves come and go over a period of several months. During this particularly vulnerable time we need long periods of quiet. It is not always possible to find a quiet environment during this fragile phase of the healing process, so be gentle with yourself. As the older swan suggests, make a clear plan for finding safe,

nurturing ways to allow the tears to continue their healing work once they begin to flow.

For example, if you know your emotions are about to be assaulted by an environment of noise and confusion, such as a large airport, try wearing dark glasses and a hat. If the tears begin while you are walking, no one will notice. If you feel the need to retreat while waiting for your flight, you can always tip the hat over your face. People will assume you are sleeping and you may be spared from engaging in unwanted conversations.

As another example, if you suddenly begin crying in the grocery store, you can always leave your cart and go to your car for a while. If you have small children, tell them about this plan so they will go with you willingly.

Do not hide your sorrow from your children. If you feel embarrassed remember, it is *essential* for children to observe their parents expressing their emotions in a healthy way.

Most people who are recovering from a personal tragedy must return to work or school before they are emotionally ready to do so. In situations such as these, it is important to make a plan for the release of these overwhelming emotions, and to make this plan known to those around us. Your plan might be as simple as asking a handful of confidants if they would be willing to take over should you suddenly need to leave the room. Confiding in a few well chosen people in this manner may be helpful to all concerned; in addition to helping you, it may allow others to feel free to ask for the same kind of support when hardship strikes their homes.

Remember that the most challenging phase of the recovery process can come four to six months after the tragedy. This difficult period may be when you need outside support the most. It may take a few years to regain your full strength following a significant loss. The progress may not seem apparent day to day. Some days will be much better than others. Two weeks may pass which seem almost normal. Then suddenly you have a day when the tears just won't leave you alone. The time it takes to heal deeply will depend upon each person's life experience. Physical age may have less influence than one may imagine. Regardless of what age we may be when our first significant loss hits, our overall needs will always be the same. We all need to feel comforted, protected, and loved.

A fifty-year-old person experiencing his first emotional trauma may take twice as long to heal as a twenty-year-old who has had more experience with significant loss. For most people, it seems that the ability to nurture others usually expedites the healing process. Studies have shown that both adults and children tend to recover more quickly and thoroughly when they can nurture other people and/or animals.

Widowed adults who were given small, manageable pets (such as kittens, ferrets, or small dogs) saw greater improvement in both *emotional* and *physical* health than those who were grieving alone. Similar results were discovered with children who were healing from divorce, a natural disaster, or a serious illness.

Most of the children I interviewed said that they felt much safer and had fewer nightmares when their pet was allowed to sleep near them during the night. (As tempting as it may be, do not give pets to adults or teenagers without their prior consultation and consent. You may find the results to be counterproductive).

In the first chapter we examined the overall traits shared by those who triumph over adversity. Now let's focus on the four key elements that seem to be consistent among these people:

- **Support**   They actively seek support inside and outside their family circle.
- **Emotions**   They honor their anger, fear, and sorrow as each emotion arises.
- **Expression** They openly express their feelings and concerns to their loved ones.
- **Time**   They respect the body's wisdom and allow the healing its own timing.

A simple way to remember this set of successful healing qualities is to use the acronym, S. E. E. T. (remember the *seet* of the soul).

People who demonstrate these qualities throughout their healing experience seem to emerge with a stronger sense of connection with life. They comment on feeling a deeper sense of rapport with their loved ones, their pets, with nature, and even with new people they meet. They also seem to demonstrate a genuine sense of compassion for themselves and others. Some of the most common life-gifts listed by those who had successfully weathered devastating storms were: a deeper sense of peace, greater appreciation for others, less fear, less anger, a deeper spiritual awareness, less anxiety, and more laughter.

Try conducting your own personal survey. Take a close look at the people in your life who have overcome adversity (especially those who absolutely amaze you. The ones with steady eyes and easy smiles). Seek these people out and tell them you would like to ask them some questions for the sake of your own healing process. You may be pleasantly surprised to find how cooperative these individuals can be.

Most people are willing to share their painful memories if they feel their experience will help someone else. Listen for the common qualities within each of their personal stories. You may be surprised how few of them use phrases like *getting tough, going it alone,* or *pulling up boot straps.*

Time after time I have found that the most admired people in any community, (those considered to be the wisest and the most authentic) have moved through the greatest difficulties in their lives by seeking support from others. Each of them took the course of **S**upport, **E**motional **E**xpression, and following the body's **T**iming (remember, the *seet* of the soul).

This on-going process of seeking support, emotional release, expressing concerns, and respecting the body's timing does not make the process any less difficult. It simply affords the best possibility for a healthy recovery.

A Note From The Author: When conducting interviews, I carefully chose individuals who were recognized by their community as being strong in character, vibrantly alive, and respected as having a sense of wisdom about them.

Each place I traveled throughout the world (no matter how stark the contrast may have been from one culture to another) when the tellers of the healing tales had easy smiles and sparkling eyes, they also had similar personality traits and shared surprisingly parallel views on overcoming adversity. In my effort to pass along their wisdom and advice I distilled the common elements of their healing stories into the *Soaring Into The Storm* parable.

We tend to remember myths and parables much better than lectures and advice. For example, if you were to logically and carefully prepare your children for the inevitability of their first emotional hurdle, when it came time to use your advice they probably would not remember the lecture.

The human brain is not designed to recall rote learning under stress, but quite easily recalls emotional connections. Thus, if the same information is offered in story form, it tends to sink into the memory at a deeper level and is usually much easier to recall when needed most — during times of emotional intensity.

The parable portion of the manuscript was released to three-hundred families for previewing prior to publication. When contacted two years later, most readers reported that the tale became part of their family's internal framework and, most importantly, influenced the way their children perceived themselves and the people they cared about.

The analogy of storms in the heart and storms in nature seemed to provide a common language for all family members and allowed them to communicate difficult emotional issues more simply and clearly.

Of the many wonderful responses we received during the previewing process, the following two are my favorites:

One family reported that their six-year-old boy responded to his grandmother's sharp tongue by gently placing his hand on her chest and saying, "Does your heart hurt inside, Grandma?" Because she was familiar with the swan parable, the grandmother was able to speak openly about her experience of being recently widowed in words her grandson could easily understand and accept.

Elizabeth, a young girl whose father was battling with a catastrophic illness, also integrated the story of the swans into her extended healing process. Over a period of several months she would often hug her mother and whisper, "My storm must be getting emptier and emptier. It doesn't hurt so much anymore."

Trouble
is part of life
and if you don't share it,
you don't give the people
who love you
the chance
to love you enough.

– DINAH SHORE

Seeking Support

"I beg you to forgive me for beginning a story that I cannot end. But the end is not yet upon my lips. It is still a love song in the wind."

– KAHLIL GIBRAN

A thin fracture in a small bone may heal on its own. A large fracture in a large bone may need experienced hands to help set it aright. The same can be true of a broken heart. Some fractures are just too severe to be left unattended.

Hearts and bones can heal *reliably*, becoming as trustworthy as an old friend, or they can heal *inappropriately*, forever limiting our freedom like an unpredictable enemy. If they are only allowed to mend on the *surface*, they may fail without any warning in the future.

If a medical professional sets your fractured bones and helps you protect them as they heal, *you* are still the one doing the healing. Similarly, if a therapist or clergy member helps you restore your fractured heart, *you* will still be the one who does the healing.

In either case, you are trusting the quality of your future to a professional. Just as in any important investment in your life, remember that you are the consumer. Shop around!

You might begin by interviewing potential therapists by phone. I would recommend asking three important questions: *How much experience have you had with these kinds of difficulties? Can you tell me about your overall approach to therapy? Have you had any personal experience in this area?* As an educational consultant over the past twenty years, I have had the opportunity to observe which therapists achieve the best results. When seeking professional assistance for yourself or your family, look for therapists who have "real" credentials. Their most *viable* credentials may be their own life experience.

If you are seeking a qualified marriage counselor, for example, choose someone who has been happily married for more than ten years. The clergy members in your place of worship may be wise and loving people, but if they are not married, you may want to seek *spiritual* counseling from them, and seek *marriage* counseling from a therapist who has more personal experience.

There will be a few rare individuals who can speak from an inner wisdom that reaches beyond personal experience. If you find an unusual treasure like this you are very fortunate. In most cases, however, the basic rule of *experience above all else* is a good one. The same rule applies to any form of support. *There is no substitute for experience.* Consider the source. Then carefully consider the substantive *quality* of the source.

For example, you probably wouldn't take any parenting advice from people who are not successful parents, or from people who have very young children (the results are not in yet!). From their first fevers to their first times behind the wheel — whenever I had vital concerns about my children's needs, I found the best advice came from the parents of happy, well-adjusted teens. These parents had the kind of obvious *real credentials* required for valuable, constructive criticism. We often overlook the obvious when seeking advice. This happens because the human brain has difficulty accessing logical thought when emotionally stressed.

Ask yourself four basic questions when taking advice from others:

1. Do they seem content in their own lives?
2. Is their *personal* experience adequate?
3. What are their credentials & references?
4. Do they demonstrate a sense of respect?

Respect is of the utmost importance. If the therapist you are interviewing does not come across as being deeply respectful of you, keep looking. *Research shows that the success of therapy has little to do with the expertise of the therapist, but a great deal to do with her values and the respect she shows her clients.**

If you choose to participate in a support group, observe the natural leaders of the group. (One or more always emerges in any group setting.) These leaders tend to set the tone for the experience of the whole. If the overall tone seems to lean toward blaming others, it may not be a safe healing environment.

When testing the waters in several support groups, you might ask yourself the four suggested questions about each group as a whole. When people are in pain, the first question *Do they seem content in their own lives?* may be somewhat inappropriate. Try replacing the first question with *Am I hearing statements of*

*Dr. Frank Pittman, M.D.,& family therapist, *Psychology Today*, Vol. 28, - 5 P 86 *personal responsibility?* Listen for an attitude of respect within the overall tone of the group. For example a statement like, *This is a wretched world and I am not going to bring any innocent children into it!* might indicate their need to blame others, or their underlying belief that no one can be trusted. This statement is very different from one like, *I just feel completely overwhelmed right now. At times, I look out at the world and I feel afraid for the children.* The latter indicates an attitude of personal power, taking responsibility for one's own feelings, and an overall belief that there are trustworthy people in the world.

Again, respect seems to be key in any successful healing experience. Respect for ourselves, respect for others, respect for the life we are living, and respect for the world which supports that life, all play an important role throughout the healing process. If these attitudes of respect are not carried by the people who are assisting you in your quest, you may want to distance yourself from them while you are healing.

Fear and blame are different faces of the same creature. Fear is always hiding behind blame. Sometimes the fear can be difficult to uncover. Other times it can be completely transparent. It is usually transparent when it is coming *toward* us. It is often much more difficult to uncover when it is coming *from* us.

My fears,
those small ones
that I thought so big

for all the vital things
I had to get and to reach.

And yet, there is only
one great thing:
to live to see in huts
and on journeys

The great day that dawns,
and the light that fills
the world.

— INUIT SONG

Healing Trauma From the Past

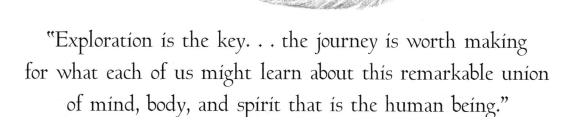

"Exploration is the key. . . the journey is worth making
for what each of us might learn about this remarkable union
of mind, body, and spirit that is the human being."

– BILL MOYERS from, *Healing And The Mind*

Sometimes a past trauma will leap from the unconscious like a wild fish, defiantly slapping the unsettled water in expanding ripples before submerging once again. The trick is to catch the slippery thing while it is still gasping for breath in the open, rather than allowing it to slip back into the unconscious where it can gain new strength.

Healing trauma from the past requires tremendous courage as it often involves diving into the unconscious and meeting the illusive creature in its dwelling place. I doubt that any one of us would take this journey were it not for the unmistakable freedom we find on the other side. I found this true while interviewing former prisoners of war,

individuals recovering from violent crime, and others who had triumphed over extraordinary adversity. The people whose faces were creased with the most smile lines and who appeared to be the most at ease with themselves approached past trauma with surprising similarity. They also shared parallel views on the best methods for healing deep emotional wounds effectively.

This chapter is devoted to conveying the combined counsel and advice of these remarkable people. At times the contents may seem a bit cut and dried, but a recipe can be much easier to follow when it is clear. The chapter also includes a few comparative observations from one culture to another.

Emotional wounding from the past can shape our experience of the present. It can shape the way we hold our bodies — the way we tend to walk, breathe, and think. And, most of all, it can shape the way we relate to the people we love.

The terrible truth about unresolved trauma is that even with our complete awareness of its existence, even when we absolutely forbid it to sway our behavior, we have little or no control over its unpredictable and unwanted influence.

Conversely, the *wonderful* thing about healing past emotional wounds is that little unforeseen miracles may unfold during the process. Along with the freedom from the pain and anxiety, completely unexpected results may occur such as deep relief from chronic migraines, back pain, or ulcers.

Emotional healing may produce surprising results such as dramatically diminishing addictive behaviors, curing sleep disorders, easing phobias, improving sexual enjoyment, and dissolving explosive temper problems.

Unfortunately, we do not get to *choose* from our personal list of possible bonuses along the way. But one benefit is almost always guaranteed. We will probably come away from the experience with a deeper sense of connection with our loved ones.

The desire to heal these hidden wounds usually arises in one of three ways:

1. The trauma simply emerges on its own, consumes us emotionally, and demands our undivided attention.

2. External signals cause temporary bouts with past trauma such as holidays or anniversaries, revisiting the location where the traumatic incident first occurred or (when crime is involved) facing the perpetrator in court.

3. We notice recurring unwanted patterns we want to change such as strong defensiveness to criticism, difficulty dealing with crowded places, outbursts of uncontrollable temper, recurring nightmares, or ongoing problems with personal relationships.

Suggestions From Others Who Have Healed

Do not try to heal your past trauma alone. Perhaps the most compelling reason for not attempting this journey on your own is that most people have found it very difficult to make any progress when traveling solo. You will probably get twice as far in half the time if you include others along the way. Support is essential in this kind of healing. Remember, you are not alone. Others have faced similar obstacles and have made it to the other side — and somehow their personal experience helps to ease the pain.

Group, self-help seminars are *not* recommended for trauma recovery. Those kinds of workshops can be beneficial for overall personal growth, but may do more harm than good when you are in the midst of recovering from a specific personal trauma.

If you are recovering from war-related stress you can seek professional guidance through your local Veterans Hospital. The quality of professional assistance differs from one hospital to another. Trust your instincts as you choose the situation that feels most comfortable to you (for details please see the chapter entitled *Seeking Support*). If you feel shy about asking for help, start by using the phone. You can call the hospital and simply say, *I'd like to talk to someone about a few nightmares I have been having lately.*

When healing from any violent trauma such as child abuse, criminal assault, war, or rape, consider including some form of body focused therapy in your recovery (beyond physical exercise). Remember, violence is not only recalled through the mind, but through the nerve cells of the body as well. Unless and until the trauma is healed in the body, it will probably remain active in the mind.

There are many choices available for body-focused therapy. If you choose massage therapy and feel shy about being undressed under a sheet, try requesting a therapist of the same sex. Because I am female, I always choose a female to administer my massage therapy.

There are also many forms of body therapy that do not involve removing your clothes. Some examples include: Cranial Sacral Therapy, Authentic Movement, Neuro-Linguistic Programming, Gestalt Therapy, Biofeedback and Dance Therapy. There are certainly many other forms of body work to choose from. Just keep the following things in mind when choosing the form that seems to speak to you:

- During the *initial* phases of trauma recovery it is probably best to stay away from *any* therapeutic form involving physical pain such as Rolfing or Deep Tissue Massage.
- Anyone administering any type of physical therapy should be professionally trained. Additionally, he or she should pass the test of *the four basic questions* as recommended in the chapter on *Seeking Support*. Beyond these measures, consult your body. Do you *feel* at ease?

Do not use your spouse or partner as your only source of support. You may both weaken under the strain and finally break apart. Think of *emotional* support in *physical* terms. When building a home each load-bearing wall has several sources of support to help distribute the weight. If the pressure on *one* of these sources becomes too intense, the structure may fail and cause the home to collapse. No matter how strong you feel your relationship may be, *please* keep in mind this simple load-bearing analogy. Look for additional support. Don't risk collapsing your own loving home.

Don't compromise your sleep schedule.*

Sleep deprivation during emotional turmoil can cause a lasting physical impact on the body. If you are having difficulty sleeping, get some help! You cannot heal effectively without the full cooperation of your brain. Certain functions within the brain are regenerated during sleep (and only during sleep). If you are not sleeping well, the synapses in the brain will malfunction.

Impulses in the brain travel through nerve cells called neurons. No thought can occur without traveling from one neuron to another. Loss of sleep may cause a temporary breakdown in the neural transmission process. The brain has a very difficult time accessing creative thought when it is low on sleep (allowing two dimensional thinking to take over). Sleep deprivation combined with overwhelming emotions only makes difficult matters worse. When sleep loss causes the neural transmission process to malfunction, the possibility of a nervous breakdown increases significantly. This phenomenon can lead to feelings of hopelessness and a strong belief that things will never get better.

* For further information contact: *The National Sleep Foundation,* 1367 Connecticut Avenue, NW Suite 200 Washington DC 20036

Once these feelings take hold, the body's chemistry can rapidly cascade downhill. When this happens, people with no previous history of depression may become clinically depressed (and temporarily suicidal). If you are experiencing insomnia, try resetting your internal clock by keeping a strict sleep schedule for a full week. In addition, try eliminating all alcohol and caffeine intake for fourteen days.

The body's internal rhythm is usually set by exposure to extended periods of light and dark. Darken the room where you sleep and step out into the daylight immediately after you awake. The sun will stimulate specific glands in your brain in ways that artificial light cannot. There are a number of short-term herbal and medical treatments for restoring sleep (consult your doctor), or you might try *Alpha Breathing.*

The human brain operates within four main states of consciousness or *brain waves*: Beta, Alpha, Theta, and Delta. These brain waves can be measured on an EEG machine or electroencephalograph. Scientists have learned a great deal about sleeping disorders with the help of the EEG. When sleep is difficult to achieve, we are usually in the Beta state of consciousness. *Alpha Breathing* has been clinically proven to smooth out the jagged Beta brain waves and ease the brain into a more relaxed Alpha state. While there are several schools of thought on the best way to time the Alpha breath, I prefer the simple 8-8-8-8 method: 1) Inhale slowly for eight counts. 2) Hold your breath in to the count of eight. 3) Empty your lungs eight counts. 4) Hold your breath out to the count of eight. (Don't count too slowly or it won't work!) It may help you to think of it in the shape of a square: ↑Draw the breath up eight counts. →Hold in for eight counts. ↓Let the breath down eight counts. ←Hold out eight counts. Repeat these four steps at least four times. Try it now. You can't help feeling more relaxed!

Remember that emotional needs are as basic as physical needs. When we look to the roots of each of our cultures, we find five universal external structures nurturing the emotional needs of each community member:

1. **Extended Family** to help nurture and raise the children
2. **Storytelling** as a means of teaching both young and old
3. **Respected Elders** who can be called upon for wisdom and guidance
4. **Artistic Endeavors** (including music and dance) for emotional expression
5. **A Community Circle** that meets on a regular basis.

Examine the cultural roots of your own family tree and you will discover these five basic elements feeding your native soil. These primary needs are as crucial to the *emotional* body as food, shelter, and clothing are to the *physical* body. In most cultures where these basic systems are still intact, children are safe and well-adjusted, crime is infrequent, violence among community members is negligible, and mood-altering substances are rarely abused. If these remarkable results are still occurring in some cultures today — then what can we do to create similar outcomes within our own neighborhoods? Much of the answer lies in taking a close look at the dislocation caused by the industrialization of our society, and the resulting strain on the overall family structure.

> The loss of
> external structures
> which support our internal
> emotional needs
> does not mean we
> no longer
> have these needs.
> It simply means these
> much-needed structures
> are missing.

In the United States, the larger sense of family was much stronger when neighbors were able to live in the same area for several generations. Thinking in terms of your own family, this strong community feeling was common in the recent past. During the era of your grandmother's generation (when she was a child) a strong unspoken family feeling usually encircled each neighborhood.

While there may be many factors contributing to the increasing numbers of broken families, could it be that family structures break down when vital structural supports are weakened or removed entirely? Industrialized societies, which have become highly mobile, lose the opportunity for extended family support. This puts an undue (and quite possibly unnatural) strain on the family structure as a whole.

Within the span of just six generations we have significantly altered the way we answer all of our basic survival needs. Our food, shelter, and clothing is now supplied by industrial organizations. We must acquire the money needed to pay for these items by attending schools and pursuing jobs that may take us miles away from home.

Because it has not been feasible to relocate our friends and family members each time we have moved, many important social structures have been lost along the way.

Parents have lost extended family care for their children. Children have lost the joy and safety of finding many loving laps in which to rest, many safe homes in which to play, and the wisdom and story-telling that comes from many respected elders in their lives.

Most importantly, our society as a whole has lost the emotional freedom that comes from participating in a larger sense of family.

The majority of the world's population comes from families where two parent-figures are not the norm; parental influence comes in sets of four or eight, as is the case with the extended family (mother, father, aunt, uncle, grandmother, grandfather and many close neighbors with similar family structures).

Whenever I see youngsters doing something dangerous, I respond to the children as if they were my own. Since the practice of parenting other peoples' children is not common in the United States today, I am accustomed to making a spectacle of myself. In Portugal, however, when I saw a six-year-old boy chase a ball into the street, I was delighted to find that I was one of *five* adults (two older women, one muscular young man, and an elderly gentleman) who instantly responded to the situation. The poor little lad was suddenly surrounded by five screaming strangers. I doubt he will make the same mistake twice!

It is possible to judge the overall emotional health of a country by the way its citizens (not the government, but the nation's people) respond to their children. In my husband's and my own experience, we have observed adults responding to children similarly in Portugal, Japan, Korea, Cuba, Tibet, the developed parts of China, most of Indonesia, and much of rural Thailand. Even though these countries range from underdeveloped (much of Indonesia) to completely industrialized (all of Japan), they all share a strong similarity; all family members participate in parenting the children. In each country it is common for family members to remain actively involved for several generations.

When the adults in every neighborhood respond to the children as if they were their own, the family experience spills over into the street. Children respond to everyone over fifty as a respected grandparent. Adults over the age of twenty-five are respected as parents, and everyone under twenty-five is regarded as an older sister or brother. The children are seldom unattended, because wherever they go they get love and guidance from the larger "family."

If the father or mother has poor parenting skills, problems with alcohol, or neglects the child in some way, several other "parents" are available to respond to the child's needs. Thus, the majority of the children raised in this manner reach adulthood with their emotional health intact. The confident yet respectful nature of children in extended family neighborhoods is a familiar sight to the seasoned traveler.

If you have not had the opportunity to observe this phenomenon first-hand, you may have to use your imagination. Imagine a nation of well-adjusted infants and toddlers who do not suffer from separation anxiety. Imagine having several trustworthy baby-sitters whom your children thoroughly adore. Imagine raising infants and young children without the added strain of sleep deprivation. While these possibilities are attractive to any loving parent, the ability to create such an atmosphere for our children seems almost unimaginable.

The constant need to relocate our families has caused a breakdown in the external structures which have nurtured our humanity over many generations. While our basic human needs remain the same, it can be very difficult to nurture our humanity in an industrialized world. The loss of the external structures which support our emotional needs does not mean we no longer *have* these needs. It simply means that these much-needed structures are *missing*. In their absence we have attempted to build a variety of new systems that can answer these needs within a mobile society. A few examples among many are:

The Foster Grandparent programs, Scouting, team sports, school functions, corporate retreats, service clubs (Kiwanis etc.), various support groups, and community programs within our places of worship. In terms of specific emotional healing, the Twelve Step programs are excellent examples of new timely structures successfully supporting ancient and timeless needs.

Any type of emotional healing can be challenging in today's world. Past trauma, however, tends to be the most confronting and the least understood. If you are dealing with a past trauma currently, you may find it encouraging to reminding yourself (and others) that you are a whole person who is healing, rather than a wounded person who will never be whole. As you discover the full spectrum of emotions hidden within a past wounding, you may want to surround yourself with others who have healed.

Within the confines of a support group it can be very freeing to identify yourself as a victim who has survived a devastating ordeal. Outside the boundaries of the support group, however, be aware of the way you speak about yourself. You may be inclined to identify yourself as a victim rather than the courageous person you actually are. Healing past trauma takes enormous courage (former war heroes interviewed stated that dealing with the nightmares and depression following the war took more courage than the acts of bravery for which they were decorated). Your healing process may accelerate if you are able to identify the wound without having to identify with it. For the sake of clarification, let's look at this identity issue in terms of physical healing. Identifying a physical difficulty is the first step toward treating the problem effectively.

An emotional healing begins the same way, but it may soon take an unfortunate turn toward negatively altering one's self-perception. Because our society openly honors the needs of the physical body, when our bodies get hurt we usually see ourselves as whole beings who need to heal.

On the other hand, because we as a society tend to neglect the needs of the emotional body, when we become emotionally wounded we fear others may see us as being less than whole — and rather than *identifying* the wound, we may tend to identify *with* it. If your intention truly is to heal, be careful not to identify with the wound. You wouldn't introduce yourself as a broken leg or an appendectomy. Is it actually helpful to tell people you *are* what you are healing? You are so much more than an unfortunate experience, or a negative behavior. Ask yourself, *Am I a rape victim, or am I a whole person who is recovering from a devastating, violent experience? Am I an over-eater, or am I a person who is recovering from an eating disorder?*

Possible Triggers for Emotional Turmoil

• **In some cases, past trauma can trigger emotional turmoil *many* years later.** For example, when you reach the age your parents were when they died, the birthday of that year may seem particularly solemn. Then the entire following year may be punctuated by unpredictable waves of emotion.

• **If you are recovering from the death of someone who was especially dear to you,** significant dates will be particularly difficult for the first few years. Birthdays, holidays, and anniversaries may be emotionally volatile times. If you are working away from home you might want to take some of your vacation days on these significant dates (particularly on the first anniversary of the death).

• **If you are recovering from violence,** sudden loud noises, unexpected physical contact, and visual reminders of past violence may bring on sudden surges of adrenaline accompanied by a flood of bad memories. Intrusive situations (such as a trespasser on your property) may suddenly trigger intense feelings of fear or anger. You may have trouble controlling your temper. And you may have violent tendencies yourself when you feel out of control. Consider seeking the support of a qualified therapist who has had some personal experience in recovering from violence. Remember, violence is not only recalled through the mind, but through the nerve cells of the body as well. Unless and until the trauma is healed in the body, it will probably remain active in the mind.

• **If you are recovering from childhood abandonment,** (i.e. your parents divorced or died when you were young, had an addictive behavior, or had jobs that kept them from home for extended periods of time) most of your emotional triggers will probably surface in personal relationships. Jealousy often stems from abandonment. You may constantly find fault with your partner — and use criticism to avoid intimacy, or you may tend to give-up before the relationship begins.

• **If you are healing from the death of a child**, spells of sorrow and anger may come and go over a period of several years. The type of grieving that is completely debilitating usually subsides within the first two years. Even so, bereaved parents are often surprised by sudden outbursts of emotion many years after their child has died.

• **If you are recovering from an addictive behavior,** try enrolling in a Twelve Step program. An addiction is not you. It is something that is hurting you. There need be no shame in seeking guidance. *Get yourself to a Twelve Step program.* No matter what your considerations may be about these programs, *they work*, and are highly recommended by *millions* of people who have successfully overcome their former addictions.

Some Clues That May Lead You To Freedom

Anytime your emotional response is greater than the current incident itself, you are probably responding to the past. Repeating that statement several times with your eyes closed can help you establish it in your long-term memory. Try it now. If you can remember this concept when you need it most, you will have access to tremendous freedom in the future.

You might also modify the statement to include others: *Anytime the emotional response is greater than the incident itself, he (or she) is probably responding to the past.* The past to which they are responding may be as recent as an hour ago or as distant as many years ago.

There is no point in attempting to uncover the source of someone else's over-reactive behavior patterns. Searching for the origin of another person's strong emotional response is a bit like entering someone's home uninvited and frantically rearranging their furniture. You can expect to be screamed at and chased down the street! No matter how close your relationship may be, *do not tread on this volatile ground uninvited.* Simply knowing that disproportionate emotional responses probably stem from the past will help you both enormously. We each have predictable patterns of behavior that are inappropriate under certain circumstances. After reviewing the following list of a few possible examples, try thinking of at least one example in your own life. Ask yourself, *What type of recurring, excessive response do I have to certain predictable situations?*

If your employer screams in your face when you make a small mistake, he or she is reacting to something other than your small error. That type of strong emotional response is appropriate for someone who is in danger. Unless the mistake you made actually put your employer (or the business) in danger, he or she probably is not responding to you.

If your spouse walks away from you during a heated argument and you respond by curling up and trembling, you probably are not responding to him or her. That type of emotional response is appropriate for a child who has just been abandoned.

If your girlfriend insults you and you are temporarily unable to speak or think, you probably are not responding to her. That type of response is appropriate for a pre-verbal child who has just been scolded.

If your neighbor becomes irrational and emotional while accusing you of building your fence several inches onto his property, he probably is not responding to you. That type of response is appropriate for someone whose personal boundaries have been violated previously (most likely during his youth). If the situation is reversed, be careful not to unload years of outrage on an innocent bystander.

Once you know this concept in your bones you will be freed from misdirected blame. When in the midst of an extreme emotional response you find yourself thinking, *I am not responding to them* or *They are not responding to me*, the energy you once used for defensiveness can be redirected toward personal freedom.

Consider the experience of Mr. D. Esfandi who is healing from war-related past trauma with extraordinary wisdom and clarity. When he was a young boy in Iran he was surrounded by a large, loving, extended family and the joy of many close friendships.

With the onset of the fighting with Iraq the Iranian government gave him two choices: kill the enemy or we will kill you. "...But I didn't see any enemy, just families they wanted me to kill. My dearest friend from high school had been arrested for his belief in democracy, and they [the government] tortured and killed him because he would not change his views. So you can see why I did not want to fight in this war. I had to escape my country quickly.

"One of the most emotional memories for me was when a very loving Kurdish family hid me in their home. They were an extremely poor family of four with two small children. They gave me the best food and clothes they could possibly offer and then sent me with a guide to cross the mountains to the border. When we were a little way up in the hills I heard shooting and screaming in the village below. My guide knew the town well and he said they [the Iranian police, as an example to the neighbors] had just killed that family and burned their house because they helped me.

"I was just a kid. It was very hard to deal with. There was nothing I could do. It was too late to go back and help them. So much love and life lost in an instant, and this was the kind of thing the government wanted *me* to do! I couldn't make myself do something like that....You can't just stop and feel the totality of what you are feeling in times like that. I had no choice. I had to keep moving.

"Too many terrible things happened. It would take a long time to list them all. There was sorrow yes, but you must deal with that later because the fear is so intense that it outweighs everything else. You have to be completely alert all the time, even in your sleep.

"Every minute of every day and night [for more than 1000 consecutive days] I knew they could find me. I looked death in the face *many, many* times. There were times that I had made my way all the way across the border [through the mountains on foot, past armed guards] only to be betrayed and returned for execution.

"People can be deceiving. You have to be on your guard. Just when you feel you are safe the whole thing turns inside out, and nothing is the way it seemed. I was sold back to the police twice by people I trusted in Turkey, *just for the money!*

"There were times I was so hungry and so far from my family....It took three years and all the money my family could get to me to finally make it to America with fifty dollars left. I used the last of my money to rent a small room. I got a job washing dishes and washed every dish with great joy! Even now [15 years later] I am thankful for my freedom *every single second!* That is why you see this big smile on my face. Still, I have some trouble trusting in personal relationships. It is getting better all the time, but it has been very difficult for me to get my trust back to the way it was in my youth, before those years of constant fear and betrayal."

Anytime
the emotional response
is greater than
the current incident itself,
we are probably responding
to the past.

When You Need to Laugh Again

"Those who don't know how to weep with their whole heart
don't know how to laugh either."

– GOLDA MEIR

There are two great mistakes we can make during times of tremendous hardship: one is to restrain ourselves from letting the tears flow, the other is to feel guilty when we laugh.

During times of personal loss, you may feel disloyal when you laugh. Yet if you did not allow yourself to laugh or smile at all, you might not survive the ordeal. If you cry "too much" at a funeral, someone in the crowd is certain to respond judgmentally. If you laugh "too soon" following misfortune someone will judge you as being shallow, insincere, or disloyal.

Unfortunately, cultures who have lost their external grieving signals (black arm bands, etc.) tend to be judgmental toward people who are grieving, or overcoming *any* form of adversity.

These judgments are fearful responses from people who have not yet gained a strong sense of balance with the losses in their own lives. When you are dealing with judgments such as these, try thinking of the people who are delivering the comments as having lost their own balance, *literally*. Imagine them on a tight-rope flailing their arms desperately to keep from falling. (This image helps me to be a bit kinder in response to their unwanted advice.)

If you find you are being judged for not crying enough, crying too much, or laughing too soon, you might try saying something like, *Well, we all find our own personal way through the darkness. Don't we? What is right for me may not be the best choice for you and vice versa.*

During the healing process we sometimes just *need* a good laugh but can't seem to muster one on our own. A collection of suggestions from some of the people interviewed follows:

- Watch kittens play. You can't *help* but laugh when kittens are having fun!

- Rent three funny movies and watch them all right in a row — not the ones you think may be funny, the ones you know will make you laugh.

- Spend time with very young children.

- Read any book by Dave Barry.

- Listen (actually *listen*) to the lyrics of country-western songs on the radio.

- Take a friend to a modern art museum and try *not* to laugh.

- Call the psychic hot-line and say you are thinking of a number between 1 and 10.

- Watch the British Parliament in session.

- Invite a close friend over and create your own subtitles to a funny foreign movie.

- Learn every last word to your favorite country or rock & roll song, and then do a lip-sink performance for your family.

- Rent the movie classic, *Harvey*

- Ask an old friend to remind you of the most embarrassing things you have ever done.

- Better yet, ask her to remind you of the most embarrassing things *she's* ever done!

- Go to a large construction site and say *I am conducting a survey on the feminine side of the carpenter's inner child. . . May I ask you a few quick questions?*

- Invite your closest friends to come to your house for an evening of charades.

- Read anything by Erma Bombeck

- Ask the toughest guy you know to do you a big favor — one that will really cheer you up. Ask him to sing "My Favorite Things" from *The Sound of Music* for you.

The look on his face alone should be enough to make you laugh! If he is a very good friend, he may actually *do* the number for you. Then you can be certain you both will be in stitches. (Have the lyrics ready just in case).

- Plan the perfect pranks to pull on your friends — ones that will really make them laugh. Even if you don't have the strength to execute your plans right away, developing a plot to bring a burst of surprised laughter to a friend is *sure* to bring a much-needed smile to *your* face.

In response to my request for chuckles in this section on comic relief, readers recommended the following country western song titles:

- I Was Lookin' Back To See If You Were Lookin' Back To See If I Was Lookin' Back To See If You Were Lookin' Back At Me

- I'd Rather Have A Bottle In Front Of Me Than A Frontal Lobotomy

- Walk Out Backwards Slowly So I'll Think You're Walking In

- Thank God And Greyhound She's Gone

- Just Drop Kick Me Jesus Through The Goal Posts Of Life

- I've Got You On My Conscience But At Least You're Off My Back

- If I Said You Had A Beautiful Body Would You Hold It Against Me?

- If You Don't Believe I Love You Just Ask My Wife

While we are taking a good look at laughter, let's look at the possibility of laughter as an aid in healing. After all, the world took a second look at the saying *Laughter is the best medicine* when Norman Cousins published his autobiographical story about over-coming a catastrophic illness by repeatedly viewing movies that kept him laughing.

"Let the world know
you
as you are,
not as you think
you should be,
because sooner or later,
if you are posing,
you will forget
the pose,
and
then where are you?"

– FANNY BRICE

If you are healing from a serious illness laughter may *be* the best medicine. If you are healing from a serious emotional trauma, however, laughter alone just isn't enough to make the medicine complete. An authentic mix of emotional release seems to make the most effective long-term remedy — emotional release including sorrow, joy, and anger.

Humanity In The Work-Place

"Loneliness is the most terrible poverty."

–MOTHER TERESA

Police, firefighters, emergency medical technicians, mental health professionals, and hospital personnel deal with traumatic events on a daily basis. People who work in fields such as these must become masters of internal emotional manipulation. Even though adrenaline may be surging through their veins, they must constantly repress these emotional signals and focus their attention on the task at hand.

The ability to stifle emotions in emergency situations is imperative to the well-being of all concerned. Yet, we now know *releasing* these harbored emotions is equally important to the overall physical and mental health of any human being. While it is clearly inappropriate for a professional to cry when responding to an emergency, it may be *very* appropriate to allow the sorrow and frustration to emerge once the emergency is over.

In most professional settings, crying is viewed as a weakness. Ironically the absolute opposite may be true. Psychologists and scientists are discovering that the continual *repression* of human emotions may actually *cause* emotional and physical weaknesses. As we have learned through numerous medical studies, emotional tears perform an excretory function.

Tears contain a number of hormones that are generated during stress. Weeping may be the most thorough and efficient way for the body to rid itself of stress-induced substances — substances that will either find their way out of the body, or remain in the system and potentially cause harm. Unfortunately, when these stress-induced hormones are allowed to accumulate and are *not* released through tears, they may adversely alter the physical, emotional, and mental capabilities of the entire body.

A police officer or medical professional who observes a young colleague crying might respond to the situation by making statements such as *Don't let it get to you!* or *You have to have a thick skin to make it here.* Well-meaning responses such as these are quite common among seasoned professionals who experience high levels of stress in the work environment. Perhaps this is why professionals who continually repress their emotional responses are more prone to alcoholism, divorce, sleeping disorders, health disorders, emotional breakdowns, post traumatic stress syndrome, and suicide.

It is unfortunate when our communities lose their qualified professionals to job-related personal crises. If these same individuals were trained to expect to feel "out-of-control" from time to time, it might be easier for them temporarily to relinquish "control" and express these uncomfortable emotions before their own personal crisis occurs. On-going training of this nature might additionally reduce the risk of job-related misdirected anger.

Firefighter, Jeanette Hentze, (a mother of two) is trained in *Critical Incident Stress Debriefing*, a system designed to help emergency response teams cope with work-related stress. She releases tension through tears, but notices that her male colleagues have a difficult time crying. Recently, she wept deeply after returning from an emergency call during which she and her partner were unable to revive a young woman who had suddenly collapsed at home in the presence of her son.

*"I'd never dealt with a child watching his mother die. That hit home. And by crying, I was able to let it out. I felt a load had been lifted. If more of my male co-workers could cry, I don't think they'd have the long-term effects of bottling up their feelings. It's better than going on a drinking binge, which definitely happens."**

Imagine a mandatory educational seminar for the immediate family members of professionals who are exposed to traumatic situations—a training which helped families identify the first signs of cumulative stress. Imagine each hospital, fire department, and police force, having a designated staff-room for the release of pent-up emotions.

If an on-going team support system were in place within each of these organizations, perhaps the people we depend on to keep us safe and healthy would lead safer and healthier lives themselves.

Perhaps it is time we stopped feeling ashamed about allowing ourselves to "break down and cry." If we do not break down our resistance to tears when the sorrow is new, the forgotten sorrow may break us down later.

*Kopecky, Gini, Redbook, vol 179 p.106(4)

If you work in a field which naturally elevates your body's stress-related hormone levels such as health care, mental health, hospice, or any emergency response profession, you may find the following sections of this book particularly helpful: *Turning the Tide, How Do We Support Each Other, Healing Trauma From the Past,* and *The Additional Research Section.* The *Critical Incident Stress Debriefing* training is designed for emergency response professionals. The training's basic structure, however, might be altered to fit your professional needs. Consult your local fire chief for more information.

Suggestions for Emotional Support Systems

Designated Peer-counseling Teams
Employees are randomly divided into teams of two members each. These teams utilize two main support systems on an on-going basis:
1. The Weekly Sounding Board. Each team (of two) meets separately once a week for a "sounding board" lunch. They meet in a setting where they will not be disturbed (such as an empty staff room with a do not disturb sign on the door — restaurants are too disruptive). Each team member has 20 minutes to speak about work-related stress while the other member listens silently.
2. Support Partners. Each member vows to be available to the other on a 24-hour on-call basis in case of an extreme emergency — those times when a work-related situation causes overwhelming emotions to arise such as dealing with a child molester, or when a parent dies and you must be the one to tell the child.

Trust & Confidentiality

Trust and confidentiality are the two main components needed to keep peer-counseling teams active and effective.

One way to begin establishing trust is by doing a simple exercise where one team member takes ten minutes to describe two memorable moments in his or her life — the most horrible, and the most wonderful. The other team member listens without interrupting. Then the roles reverse. Once you have shared experiences which are so private and so dear, you will find your judgments about each other begin to dissolve, while your mutual trust begins to solidify.

Confidentiality can be ensured by co-workers maintaining the golden rule of the safe work environment, and openly refusing to engage in gossip. Confidentiality can be reinforced by violators risking the possibility of strong disciplinary action following any flagrant violation.

Note: You will find other low-cost and no-cost suggestions for establishing or enhancing emotional support systems in the workplace in the *Soaring Into The Storm Workbook* (See the order forms in the back of this book.)

If you are an employer in a high-stress work environment and you do not have emotional support systems in place for yourself and your employees, consider the benefits you may be denying yourself. Emotional support systems can be low-cost or no-cost. Additionally, they help to *increase* loyalty, productivity, teamwork and a community atmosphere, while *decreasing* resentment, misdirected work-related anger, absenteeism, and employee turnover.

If you are an employee in a high-stress work environment where there are no emotional support systems in place, create some! Offer to do some research on the subject. Most employers would welcome some volunteer support to improve the quality of their work environment.

Imagine what your relationship might be like if your spouse no longer had to be your emotional dumpster after work. Imagine how your parenting skills might increase if you were less tired and more relaxed when you were home. (Isn't it amazing how much our children's behaviors improve when we are relaxed?)

There are other possible bonuses—when stress-related toxic substances in the body *decrease*, sexual desires and sexual performance levels often *increase*. This is a wonderful point to bring up when dealing with a tough-as-nails co-worker who is trying to find the courage to release emotions his society calls "unmanly."

People
who work
in fields such as these
must become masters
of internal
emotional manipulation.

. . . We now know that
releasing these harbored
emotions is important to the
overall physical and mental
health of every human being.

While it is clearly
inappropriate
for a professional to cry when
responding to an emergency,
it may be *very*
appropriate
to allow the sorrow
and frustration to emerge
once the emergency is over.

Supporting Others Through An Illness

"There is a bridge between time and Eternity. . .
This is the bridge of the human spirit."

– FROM THE UPANISHADS

There are many wonderful books available for people who are overcoming the challenges of a serious illness. Therefore, in this chapter we will focus entirely on their care-givers. I would like to point to three general areas of concern for those who are supporting their friends or loved ones through this heart breaking ordeal:

1. Delegating responsibilities
2. Dealing with fear and projections
3. Allowing the heart to speak

Delegating Responsibilities

From the first moment you receive the diagnosis, delegate, delegate, delegate! Serious health management takes a lot of time. Regardless of which healing avenue you may take, you will need hours and hours to simply focus on the unforeseen, unpredictable, logistical details involved. Time will be the most difficult thing to find, so seek it out. Give away the things that matter the *least* so you have time for the *people* who matter *most*. This is no time to be shy. Delegate your yard work, pet care, laundry and house cleaning. Delegate much of your business activity. Don't worry about having to pay for these services. Delegate people to delegate. Tell two of the most organized people you love that you need them to come over, have dinner, and help you organize your life. (Then ask them to bring the dinner!)

By delegating your responsibilities you will be better able to your maintain your sleep schedule. If you consistently hold your sleep as sacred, the experience will be rich with authenticity. If you deprive yourself of sleep, you may become short-tempered, regret your behavior, and find it difficult to be yourself.

Don't be shy about asking for assistance from friends and co-workers. They may be helplessly waiting to be asked. If you get an unfavorable response, ask someone else. Whenever you begin to feel self-conscious, or embarrassed, recall how helpless you felt when someone you loved became ill and there was nothing you could do. If a family member had asked you to help in a specific way, such as mowing the lawn occasionally, or vacuuming on Saturdays, how would you have responded?

Delegating In The Hospital

If you are dealing with hospital care try to have a *patient advocate* on duty — someone who can provide for the ill person's physical needs, and help with communications between the patient and the health care professionals. The position can be shared between several close friends and family members. It is very helpful to have each advocate make a few notes in the same daily, on-going journal. This eliminates the need to communicate by phone or in person when advocates are changing shifts.

An advocate can do several simple things to make the hospital stay more tolerable such as providing ice or fluids on a regular basis, straightening out the bed, reading aloud to the person who is ill, and quietly answering the phone when the patient is sleeping. He or she can also help to avoid difficulties should a health care professional become over-tired. Some hospitals still force doctors and nurses to work long shifts without sleep. Errors and misunderstandings happen more frequently when people are sleep-deprived.

Be kind to your health care professionals. You will find most of them to be dedicated, competent people, and they certainly are not to blame for a ridiculous (and unhealthy) policy of long, sleepless shifts.

If your loved one is losing sleep due to the unfamiliar noises in the hospital, try using headphones and listening to white noise while you sleep (the sound of the ocean is my personal favorite). You can overcome the distractions of hospital odors by dabbing some attractive smelling lip balm directly underneath the nose. Lip balm outlasts perfume and is less intrusive.

If you are supporting your child or your spouse through an illness, in most cases you can arrange to snuggle in the hospital bed together from time to time. Don't let anyone tell you otherwise. Even if it is only for a few minutes a day, snuggle close and drink in the pure unspoken nurturing that heals the soul. It will help you both on a very deep level. So insist!

I speak from personal experience. My son and I wove our way through oxygen tubes, I.V. tubes, and heart-monitor wires everyday during his ten weeks in serious condition. He died in my arms several times, but always returned. Now he is a gorgeous man who threatens to pick me up and carry me to the car whenever I embarrass him in public. Our ordeal had a glorious outcome. Yet, even for those families whose long journey ends in death, the ability to enjoy the quiet intimacy of physical closeness seems to ease the pain for all concerned.

Carolyn Wheatley's husband, Mike (a medical doctor himself), was diagnosed with cancer and died a few weeks later. Even though her husband was extremely familiar with the medical environment, and the people providing for his care were his own friends and colleagues — he found his hospital stay nearly unbearable. One of Carolyn's fondest memories of the experience came when they were snuggling in his hospital bed together. She said, smiling tearfully, "Slowly he turned, kissed me, and then whispered, *When you hold me all of this disappears and I can just float on a cloud of your love.*"

If you are arranging for some hospice support at home, rent two hospital beds that can be placed side by side. If you feel your financial situation might be strained by renting two beds, ask your closest friends to sponsor a simple fund-raiser (a sports event, a bake sale, a neighborhood garage sale, a no-talent show, a dance, a raffle, the possibilities are endless).

Dealing With Fears & Projections

Be on the watch for panic in disguise. It will surround you and your family. A number of friends, acquaintances, and even family members will be deeply shaken when illness or death circles too close to their own lives. This is a human phenomenon that cannot be avoided. A certain degree of fear is stirred in all of us when the harsh reality of illness or death suddenly dominates our lives. We fear two things: *This could happen to me*, and/or *This could happen to someone I love.* The experience touches two primal fears: our fear of the unknown, and our fear of being left alone.

Everyone will try to figure out how the illness (or accident) happened and how it could have been avoided. We can't help ourselves. When the human brain senses danger it automatically tries to locate the predator and map out an escape route. An emotionally *mature* person will go through this process mentally, and then proceed to support the family in crisis. An emotionally *immature* person will go through the process verbally (in some cases repeatedly) and then proceed to add his or her panic to the family's unfortunate situation.

Disguised panic can be draining at its best and, at its worst, may be dangerous. It comes in many forms. Perhaps the most benign panic comes cloaked in the form of smiling cliches, and the most dangerous comes in the form of a blaming child hidden in an adult body. An example of the former: *Don't be upset. It is all for the best. There is no reason for sorrow.* An example of the latter: *He/She is ill because of_____. If it wasn't for_____, none of this would be happening!* Responses such as these may be appropriate for a child, but when an adult responds in this manner it is usually a cry for help. No matter how much you may feel pulled to respond to the needs of these people, or feel compelled to help them grasp the reality of the situation, *save it for later.* Time is a precious commodity for any family wrestling with a serious illness.

Neither the care-giver nor the one currently needing care can afford to spend their waking hours dealing with other people's fears. Whether the panic is wrapped in a happy cliché or delivered in blame, the body language carries similar characteristics: The torso leans too far forward. The voice seems to be too loud. The eyes often seem to disagree with the message the mouth is delivering; and the whole body seems to carry some sense of urgency. In other words, these people are far too concerned about getting their point across. It seems as though they are trying to convince *themselves* of what they are saying.

Should they be forgiven? Absolutely! Should their fears be addressed? Most certainly! (somewhere else). Should they be allowed to be near the care-giver or the individual who is ill?

Only if absolutely necessary and, even then, the visit should be brief. Make a note of these people's names in the patient-advocate journal so their visits can be kept to a minimum. (Just the name and a star will do. Any simple code of this nature will allow you to keep the information confidential.)

Another unfortunate fear response may come in the form of a sudden disappearing act by someone you love. Please don't be surprised if one of your closest friends pulls away. He or she is simply overcome with fear. If you let this behavior hurt you, your heart will be doubly broken — once for the difficulties your loved one is facing, and again for the loss of a close friendship.

Dealing with inappropriate responses is an unavoidable challenge faced by all care-givers. If the people making these inappropriate comments are close friends or family members, try taking them aside and telling them that they are unintentionally creating discomfort. Tell them you understand what they are really trying to say is *I love you.* Remind them that each heartfelt *I love you* is worth a million words.

> Neither the care-giver nor the one currently needing care can afford to spend their waking hours dealing with other people's fears.

Things you can say to people who are making matters worse:

- He had a restless night and we both need to catch-up on sleep for a couple of days. Thank you for coming. I know he appreciates your show of support.

- She is feeling a bit overwhelmed by visitors lately, but I will tell you what you *can* do. Could you please go to the library and check out some more talking books for her? She is truly enjoying listening to them when she can't sleep.

- Could you please read aloud from his favorite book? He has been enjoying reading so much more than conversation lately. It helps him forget about the illness for a while.

- She has requested some quiet time for reflection for a few days. The written word is the best way to offer your love to her right now. She just lights up when the mail comes in.

- He is in a vulnerable state right now. We are limiting his personal visits in an effort to build-up his immune system. Let's just give him a week or so to gain the strength he needs to deal with this.

- She is listening to some soothing music with headphones right now. Would you like me to see if she would enjoy having you rub her back *gently and quietly?*

Things you can do to help save your energy for the ones you love:

- Get an answering machine for your published number and turn off the volume and the ringer. Then get a new unpublished number and only give it to your immediate family members and very close friends.

- Place a sign outside that says, *Shhh Sleeping Now. Please, no visitors for So-&-So today.* Then people won't come through the door unannounced. You can also do this in the hospital so long as you stick your sign on the door with something called Fun-tak. It is a reusable adhesive by DAP ™ (available at most hardware stores).

- Go through scrapbooks or photo albums and revisit your most wonderful memories aloud. It will take you and your loved one on a healing journey into the joys of life you have shared in the past, and provide some welcome distraction in the present.

- Eat well. People will ask if there is anything they can do for you. Don't be shy about asking for good food. It is one of the few things most people feel very comfortable about giving. Be specific. Ask for lots of energizing juices and protein rich snacks. Ask for orders "to go" from affordable restaurants...and, now and then, ask for your favorite dessert.

Letting The Heart Speak: Very few of us move though the stages of illness or death without slipping into a dream-like state of consciousness. These extremely vivid daydreams are sometimes caused by pain medication. Other times they are simply a symptom of the illness itself. For most of us, however, they are a natural (and perhaps very important) part of the dying process.

Most of the family members I interviewed expressed deep regret for trying to reorient their disoriented loved ones. The response seemed to be quite universal. When the loved ones finally realized they were not fully conscious, they felt deeply embarrassed, fearful of losing their sanity, depressed, and feared they had become burdensome to others. Few of them ever returned to their previous calm state of self-confidence unless or until the illness was cured.

In contrast, the families who sailed through these uncharted waters with a greater sense of ease simply jumped in the boat and joined in the journey. If their loved ones became frightened, rather than denying the experience, they said, *You are having a nightmare!* and implored the dreamer to awake. If their loved one was content with the dream journey, the family followed. For example, a young man whose mother kept returning to her college days often asked her son if he had seen a particular person on campus. When he replied, *No I haven't, have you?* The conversation usually circled back to the present. As another example, a young woman's dear grandfather repeatedly pointed to the window and said, *There they are again!* When she asked, *Who are they?* He replied, *I think they must be angels!* These joyful words eventually became a great comfort to her. He died shortly thereafter.

. . .It is not thought
that answers each step
of my feet. . .
I am so stained with the
sweet peculiar loveliness of things
that given God's power
to dream worlds from the dark,
I know I could only
dream Earth
– birds, trees, this field of light
where I and each of us
walk once.

–JOHN DANIEL excerpt from *Of Earth*

Interviews From Around The Globe

"Out of the night that covers me, black as the pit from pole to pole. . .
I am the master of my fate: I am the captain of my soul."

– W. E. HENLEY from *Invictus*

Publisher's note: This chapter differs from the rest as it replicates the format for *Soaring Letters,* a companion publication soon to be released. It includes a small sampling of letters and interviews focused on overcoming adversity. The youngest contributor is eight years of age, and the oldest is seventy. While the ages, personalities, and cultural backgrounds of the contributors to this section are quite diverse, common themes seem to evolve in each person's story. Some of these interviews may leave the reader feeling uplifted while others may arouse feelings of discomfort.

Therefore, *we do not recommend this section for children under the age of eleven.* On the other hand, should a younger child be having difficulties which parallel the experiences of a particular interviewee such as nightmares, taunting at school, a difficult divorce, a learning disability diagnosis, or a fearsome hallucination under anesthesia, sharing that specific information might be helpful to the child.

A RETIRED TEACHER SHARES THE BOOK with fellow senior citizens: When I first read your book, I thought how helpful it would have been to share the story of the swans with my children and grandchildren during painful times over the years. Then it occurred to me that this wonderful story would also be helpful to me and others in my age-group who are all too familiar with loss.

Those of us who are older (and supposedly wiser) sometimes deny ourselves the right to grieve openly, thinking that we must set a strong example for our family. Grieving, after all, is socially unacceptable. There seems to be an unspoken assumption that shortly after the divorce is final, the funeral is over, or the visible signs of an illness have subsided, we must pull ourselves together and move on. As your book points out, grief has its own wisdom and its own time-frame. Perhaps the time that it takes is the time that it needs, nothing more, nothing less.

In the future, if I see someone in my age group who is suffering in silence, I am going to offer them this book, rather than a sympathy card. After all, we are not alone.

Bea Kerr — Oregon, USA

A JAPANESE PHOTOJOURNALIST RECOVERS from being tortured by Serbian secret police: When I was covering the war in Bosnia I was captured by the Serbs and taken to their secret police. They stripped off my clothes and beat me for several hours, laughing. They broke my ribs. Then they left me naked in ten below zero temperatures to die alone...I think my anger kept me alive. I just wasn't going to let them win!... I was very, very angry! At the time I wanted to kill the three men who tortured me.

When I finally made it home, I thought about how much I hated them every day as I was healing. I would often remember their faces and think about how I would react if I saw one of them again. It hurt me to breathe for quite a while after the beating, so with every breath I remembered those men again.

I come from a samurai caste. This means my ancestors were trained in the samurai code of honor.... I remember I could laugh, cry, or have temper tantrums until I was seven. Then, quite suddenly, I was told I was too old to show that kind of weakness. This kind of training is not uncommon in Japan — especially among samurai descendants. Even now I often laugh at times when most of my American friends would think yelling or crying would be more appropriate. So you see, talking about this experience was not something I could easily do at home. When I was healing from the torture, I could not go out for quite a while and it took a long time before I could talk on the phone without any pain. I called my American friends as soon as I could talk. They let me say the most about terrible things like this. The Japanese have a harder time listening to upsetting feelings. I just had to talk about it. It always helps to talk about it. It feels good to have the chance to talk about it again right now.

After some time my rage healed along with my body...If I had seen one of those men several months ago I would have attacked him and beaten out my rage on him. Now that most of my anger is out, if one of them came through the door right now I know I would probably punch him a few times until I saw his weakness, and then I could not hit him any more. Every time I talk about it, it gets a little easier, and I feel a little less anger.

The experience has not influenced my feelings about the Serbian people as a whole. I met several very kind-hearted Serbs. It is just these three men I still have anger for. They were very mean people!

A note from the Author: Even as this man was describing his horrible ordeal, an overall love for others seemed to encircle him. This prompted me to ask the following question: *Most of your assignments are war-related. How do you go to work in hell so many days out of each year and still have this genuine love for life that seems to radiate from your eyes?*

This is a very difficult thing because I live with the people whose lives I am documenting. Sometimes we live together for several months and become good friends. Many, many of the people in my pictures have since suffered and died. . .very, very fine people.

I have two eyes. One of my eyes sees the anguish, pain and suffering. The other eye sees nothing but the light, the angle, and the possibility of a photograph. When I am documenting a tragedy, I close my human-eye and focus my camera-eye through the lens. When I get back home again I can open both of my eyes and integrate the depth of my experience as I review my developed prints. But when I am on the battlefield, I must always remain in the eye of the camera.

If I can keep clear-headed enough to bring back pictures of how we are hurting each other, I know I can stir the compassionate side of humans. If no one is willing to risk his life to bring back the news, then these travesties remain someone else's problem far away from here. My photographs are all I have to give. I want to take them well and make them a tribute to those who suffer... people say I am brave, but this is not the kind of bravery I admire. Facing each day with a terminal illness, to me, *that* is bravery. I don't know if I could fight that kind of battle. I don't think I could be that brave. The idea just terrifies me. *Masao Endoh—Japan*

(Mr. Endoh's work has appeared in *Time* magazine, *Life*, *Newsweek* and numerous other international publications. He has photographed nearly every violent conflict world-wide for more than twenty-five consecutive years — and works in battle zones approximately two-hundred and fifty days out of each year.)

A TEACHER FROM CHINA REFLECTS on the book: Each time I read *Soaring Into The Storm* I gain a new view of the concepts of vulnerability and strength. I admire "Young Swan" for learning these concepts and "Gray Swan" for its compassion and understanding. Good myths are equally meaningful to people of all ages and cultures. In fact, "Young Swan" is not necessarily young of age — I see the attributes of this character in my friends, colleagues and myself as I reflect on my past thirty-some years growing up, studying, teaching, and living in China.

The dominant Chinese culture often discourages individuals from releasing their emotional "storms." Nevertheless there are also subcultural rituals that encourage people to express their sorrow, just as the story suggests. I think this book will help many families in my country gain a clearer understanding of themselves, their close friends, and their loved ones.

Yanhong Zhang — The People's Republic of China

A CANADIAN BOY TALKS ABOUT HEALING from the trauma of his sister's violent death: My sister was stabbed to death by some crazy guy three years ago. At first it helped to be able to talk about it over and over again to anyone who would listen. Kids my age would talk about it and ask more questions than my parents' friends would. Also, my friends were not so afraid to cry with me. The crying was ok with them but they were afraid of my anger... I wanted to find that guy and cut him up! I felt really strong and I thought I could do it, too! I wanted *him* to see how it felt. I just kept seeing my sister dying over and over again in my mind. The story about the storms and the swans really helped. We all [his family] made a plan for getting these horrible feelings out, because sometimes it just hits you really hard in the grocery store or at school and you can feel just totally trapped. It's kind of like making a family plan for an escape route in case of a fire. Because, if you just stay there and don't do anything about it the fire will burn you up and ruin your life. The counseling really helped too. My mom and dad and I all went together. Besides talking and crying and yelling forever and ever, what helped the most was when she [the therapist] read us some interviews of people who had been stabbed and almost died, but lived instead. They all said at first they felt afraid and then it hurt only for a second. Then they said the pain left quickly, because of shock I think, and then their minds took them to a peaceful place. Some of them said that they were suddenly with the people they loved the most, and it felt like they were *really there!* It is good to know that my sister could come and be with me while she was dying because I felt very guilty that I was not with *her*. These people also said that their pain was horrible while they were healing, but not when they first got stabbed. They were surprised how soon they didn't feel anymore pain right after it happened. I am glad my sister didn't have to suffer.

Then the best thing she [the therapist] said was that we were living through the terrible part of her death over and over again in our minds and especially in our dreams, but she [the sister] only went through it once.

We are all right now but it took almost three years to get through the worst of it. Sometimes I see something my sister liked, or I hear a song she used to sing and I cry because I miss her. But this kind of crying feels really soft, it doesn't hurt like the old kind of crying did. I remember thinking that I would always cry and never ever laugh again. My mom and dad felt that way too, but we really are happy again now. It feels strange to say 'again' because we are not happy like we used to be. We are happy in a different way now. It's really hard to explain… little things that used to bother me a lot don't bother me so much anymore. People say I have a special sparkle in my eyes. So many people say that and I don't know why. Maybe it's because I have cried so much that I am so clean inside now or maybe my sister's light is shining inside of me from heaven because I still love her so much.

— *Name withheld upon request of the family.*

THE DIRECTOR OF AN ORPHANAGE IN PORTUGAL talks about helping the new children through the trauma of abandonment: Some of our children have been raised in an orphanage since they were infants, and others come to us when they are older. It is the ones who are abandoned by their families at an older age who have the hardest time.

Many of our older boys are sent here by families in poverty who just cannot afford to take good care of their children. Some of these children may have died if they had remained in their own homes. Our facility is funded by both the church and the government. We can give the impoverished boys better care here than they can receive in their former homes. The boys get good meals, good medical care, and good skills to support themselves later in life. These things may not be possible at home, so sometimes the families give up their children with great sorrow because they know it is the best choice. Nevertheless, the experience of abandonment is still very difficult for the child. It may take one or two years for him to feel at home with us and start smiling again.

Most of the rest of our children were born to teenage mothers or prostitutes. If the boys get into a fistfight it is usually because somebody said someone else was the son of a prostitute. These words can be very painful because they are often true. But fistfights rarely happen at all, just maybe twice a year.

As you can see, there is a strong feeling of family here. I think there are two keys to helping any child through life. The first key is to be a loving family. The teachers who live in the monastery, as well as the lay-teachers, are taught to talk with the boys as if they were their mother or father, not their teacher. If the boys are afraid or upset we just hold them while they cry. We hug our children often and if there is a problem we respectfully talk it over in private. We do not embarrass them in the sight of others. The second key is to help them learn good skills so they can feel proud of their work. As often as possible we involve the boys in vocational projects which many people in the community will see [such as producing printed material for business or becoming involved in construction work]. When the boys walk through town, they can see their own accomplishments and take pride in themselves and their new family. *Father Goncalves — Vila do Conde, Portugal* [As my husband and I left the Father's office we suddenly felt the warmth of the sun on our backs, even though we were still inside a windowless stone hallway within the monastery. We both turned around to find the source of this sudden warmth. The physical sensation we simultaneously experienced was somehow generated by this compassionate man as he steadily watched us walk away. It was one of those strange and wonderful unexplained experiences.]

AN EIGHT-YEAR-OLD DEALS WITH DIVORCE, a move, a new school, and schoolmates teasing him about learning disabilities: When my parents first got divorced it was no big deal because they still got along ok and we lived in the same town and I could get to my mom or my dad's house anytime I wanted to on my bike. But then my new dad took us far away because he had to go to a special training for his company. That is when the divorce really hit me because I couldn't see my father or my friends unless I flew on a plane. That didn't happen much.

My new school was awful. There was hardly any grass to play on, only cement, and no one was even very friendly to me. I had a hard time reading the assignments as fast as I was supposed to. The other kids were faster at it. I couldn't get my work done, so the teacher made me stay inside every recess to finish my work. That is when the other kids started making fun of me. I just didn't have any friends at all anymore.

One time when I came back from seeing my father I just stood in the airport and shook and cried. My mom hugged me and she cried too because she was sad for me. We had a family meeting and decided that I was going through too many changes all at once. So I got to go to a brand new private school that had small classes and real alive grass! The new school cost lots of money, so we were pretty poor for a while. But it was worth it! I still had trouble with that shivering kind of shaking sometimes though. It happened for, I think, about a month or so more, just every now and then.

The storm story really helped me get my sadness and afraidness out. I know how he felt when he was scared to death in the hail! [This interviewee imagined the young swan to be male.] Every time my body started shivering, my folks would remind me about my storm getting harder if it stayed inside, and I would let it out. So, after my dad finished up his training we moved to a new town. I felt ready to try a public school again.

They say I have 'learning disabilities' but my folks say I just have a different way of learning. My mom says that anybody different is going to be teased so you might as well be ready for it. My parents did a lot of practice with me about teasing before I went to the new public school. When I finally went to the new school I loved it!...One day the other kids were making fun of me when we were playing basketball. They were singing *Steven's a slow reader!* over and over again. I remembered about the teasing practice I did with my folks. So, I just held the ball until the game stopped and I said, *Yes, I am a slow reader. You know that, and I know that. Now are you going to waste our recess singing a stupid little kid's song, or are we going to play basketball?* Then I threw the ball really hard to the leader of the song, and the game started again. I felt like I just won a gold medal! Kids really started to respect me and they all stopped teasing me after that.   *Steven J. — USA*

A WOMAN RESOLVES SOME PAST TRAUMAS and learns why she has always hated doctors: I remembered my parents making humorous references to the time I kicked the doctor in the teeth. When I asked my mother for the details, I learned why

I had always been so terrified of doctors and dentists. Once my mother reminded me of this traumatic incident, all the forgotten memories returned in detail.

When I was five years old, my parents took me to a hospital for a tonsillectomy. I had never even seen a hospital before. I didn't know why I was there or what was going to happen to me. I remembered being taken into surgery and being put under anesthesia. The doctor was looking straight at me and holding the knife when I was strapped down and under the mask. I didn't know what was going on. I was so young that I only had the ability to think like a small child. I only knew that a bad man was trying to cut me and I couldn't hit him or run away! I wanted my parents to burst in and protect me. I felt so alone!

It must have been because I was so young and so terrified and my mind couldn't make sense of the situation, but suddenly the doctor and his staff all turned into wild animals attacking me with sharp claws and teeth. I felt completely alone, horrified and totally helpless. The next thing I remembered was waking-up in intense pain. The doctor who did the operation came to my hospital room. I knew he was the one who had hurt me. When he leaned down into my crib I kicked and screamed and kicked him in the teeth. He was very angry and yelled to my mother, 'Get that girl away from me before I kill her!' In my mind, he had already tried.

My parents used to tease me about being so strong that I could kick a doctor's teeth in. I knew it had happened, and somewhere inside I must have known about every detail of the whole experience. But, to *know* something and to *feel* it are two very different things! To actually *consciously* feel the fear and pain finally releases it! It is so illuminating! It changes the way you look and feel and act. Best of all, it changes the way you relate to the people you love.

[In an effort to foster similar experiences of freedom through personal growth, she sought the guidance of a well-respected therapist] ...There were so many other instances when I believed I was alone — so many times when I just felt like I couldn't trust anyone. One day during a therapy session, I stopped *thinking* about feeling alone and finally let the *feelings* of aloneness all the way in. That is when it *really* hit me. 'Why am I so afraid of being alone? I can be alone and take care of myself just fine!' I could feel the fear and anger melting away. I didn't think it. I felt it! It was so amazing to feel the feelings I had been thinking about for so many years. Suddenly, my hands opened up, my chest opened up, and a warm feeling came over me. It was so freeing! Sometimes we live with fears or frustrations that we could be free of if we would only ask for help.

...This same sense of nurturing support is what struck me about the swan myth. When we are suffering we need others we can depend on — not only for assistance, but for guidance. We need to hear someone else say *It's ok to feel the way you feel.* In the story the healing begins when she [this interviewee imagined Young Swan as a female] stops feeling alone and starts asking questions. She asks, 'Where does the river go?' Once she takes that first step, then her whole life begins to transform. *Cindy Young — California, USA*

Saying Good-bye To A Beloved Pet

"Grandfather Great Spirit, all over the world the faces of living ones are alike...
Teach us to walk the soft Earth as relatives to all that live."

– A SIOUX PRAYER

Our pets are important members of our families, yet we are often surprised by the depth and breadth of our grief when it comes time to say good-bye to these dear ones.

We may even feel embarrassed to admit our sorrow to others, yet denying ourselves the possibility of their comfort may be a terrible mistake. If you find yourself in conflict over the depth of your feelings, try telling yourself, *I have just lost a special member of my family.*

Farewells are never easy, especially when we must say good-bye to a love so selfless and innocent. No matter what your spiritual background may be, you might find the following Sioux prayer helpful when grieving the loss of your dear one. My family and I have whispered these graceful words at several grave sites.

Grandfather Great Spirit
all over the world
the faces of living ones are alike.
With tenderness they have come up
out of the ground.

Look upon your children that they may face
the four winds and walk the good road
to the day of quiet.

Grandfather Great Spirit
fill us with the light.
Give us the strength to understand,
and the eyes to see.

Teach us to walk the soft Earth
as relatives to all that live.

When well-meaning people encourage you to get another kitten (puppy, bird, etc.) remind them that you have lost *this* pet, and you need time to grieve *this* loss. Children need to learn appropriate ways to respond to inappropriate comments as well.

The death of a pet is often a child's first introduction to his or her inner world of deep feelings — the first emotionally charged memory. Experiences such as these set down the first neural pathways in the brain concerning adversity. Thus, the first grieving experience may play a significant developmental role.

Due to the way the human brain develops, scientists speculate that childhood experiences may influence the formation of the personality by as much as 70%. If adults minimize a youngster's first conscious experience of extreme emotion, the child may learn to minimize emotional feelings in the future. Our children will face many experiences of loss as they grow older, and eventually they must learn to endure without our guidance. As difficult as it may be, the tragic death of a pet can also serve as an opportunity to help our children build healthy coping skills.

Here are a few simple suggestions for ways you may want to pay tribute to your beloved pet :

- Read the parable of the swans aloud together shortly after the pet dies, and then once again two or three weeks later. Ask the questions recommended in the *Using This Unusual Book* section.

- As the old swan suggests, make a plan for how you will release your sorrow should it arise in different situations.

- Prepare appropriate responses to possible inappropriate comments from others.

- Talk about your memories: *Remember when kitty did this or that? What I will miss most is....*

- Make a gift for the animal, or write a letter of appreciation and fond farewell, then bury these things at the grave-site.

- Have some kind of burial ceremony and clearly mark the grave site. Then, if you (or your child) are having a particularly difficult day missing your pet, you can visit the grave — just as you would with any beloved friend or family member.

> Carefully observe what way your heart draws you and then choose that way with all your strength.
>
> – HASSIDIC SAYING

Shielding Children From Adversity

"Be like the forces of nature. When it blows, there is only wind.
When it rains, there is only rain. When the clouds pass,
the sun shines through."

— LAO TZU, Ancient Chinese Philosopher

It is natural for us to want to protect our children from exposure to danger and pain. However, protecting children from their own *emotional* pain can be counterproductive to their overall development. Emotional pain will find its avenue of release sooner or later — sometimes *years* later.

Contrary to popular parenting responses such as *Be brave!* or *Don't be a crybaby!*, most mental health professionals agree that encouraging children to let their tears flow may actually keep them from becoming "crybabies" later in life. In clinical studies, most adults who cried *inappropriately* (in response to constructive criticism or under low levels of stress) had developed a low sense of self-esteem during their childhoods. On the other hand, those who had developed a solid sense of self-esteem during childhood also cultivated a strong sense of respect for the full spectrum of their emotions while they were young. (See *Additional Research*.)

All children will experience trauma and loss at some point in their lives. Pets will get lost, dear friends will move away, and young hearts will be broken. Eventually, our children will have to say good-bye to someone very dear. Unfortunately, we cannot predict when a child's first significant loss will occur. Perhaps it will happen at the age of seven when a beloved family pet dies, at the age of nine when a close family friend is diagnosed with a catastrophic illness, or at the vulnerable age of fifteen when burgeoning love is devastated for the first time.

Our children will have to learn to navigate their way across the channels of sorrow, just as they must learn to navigate their own way across the street. As in most learning situations, children begin by holding our hands and following our guidance until they master the skills on their own.

I recommend reading *Soaring Into The Storm* aloud to children when they experience their first significant loss. If we share the story of the swans with our children during their *first* loss, they will gain some of the important skills needed when facing larger storms later in life.

If the parable were to be condensed into one sentence it would be, *Honor the wisdom of the body's timing.* This concept is particularly important when dealing with children in crisis. A childhood trauma may resurface on various developmental levels over a period of several years. While it is important to encourage children to release their emotions, it can be equally important to respect the wisdom of their bodies and not attempt to pull the feelings out prematurely. There is a respected old saying that the Lord never gives us more than we can handle. The same can be said of the unconscious, or the *psyche*.

In cases of extreme trauma (such as a natural disaster, witnessing or experiencing violence, sexual molestation, or when recovering from multiple traumas such as successive family tragedies) the psyche may block the original overwhelming memories until the ego is strong enough to deal with them. This is why it is so important to *follow*, rather than *lead* the child. For example, if a child is angrily beating a punching bag and then suddenly stops, it is better to ask, *Is that enough for now?* than to say, *I know you have more anger in there! Get it all out of your system!* If we break down a child's defenses, we may be literally breaking down the child. If you are uncertain about how to *follow* rather than *lead* your child's healing process, try this two-phase technique:

1. Always phrase your concerns in the form of a question, *Do you need a hug? Is it time to cry? Would you like to do some artwork? Do you have some other ideas about how to get these feelings out?*

2. Imagine you are speaking to a wise old gate-keeper inside your child — one much older and wiser than yourself. Regardless of what your own desires may be, the child's internal gate-keeper knows best.

> When we break down a child's defenses, we may be literally breaking down the child.

Guiding Children Through Turmoil

"Children require guidance and sympathy far more than instruction."

– ANN SULLIVAN, Helen Keller's childhood teacher.

One of the best things we can do when our children are hurting is to tell them it makes us feel sad when they are sad. It is also important to let them know they will have some good days and some extremely difficult days. But, little by little, they will heal; and although it may be difficult to believe right now, they *will* feel good again.

A child's recovery from trauma may differ from an adult's in several ways. Two of the most significant in my opinion are the following:

- Their tendency to have unrealistic fears about their own safety and the safety of others.
- Their tendency to distrust the world as a whole.

These tendencies can remain *temporary* or develop into more *permanent* aspects of our children's personalities, depending upon our response to their needs. The first six months following a tragedy are the most crucial.

All children have four basic needs in order to heal in a healthy manner:

1. **Love**
2. **Emotional Release**
3. **A Quiet Place** in which to retreat alone (both at home and during school hours).
4. **Consistency** in their physical world and in their daily routine. (This is not the time to change their bedtimes, offer new challenges, or redecorate their rooms.)

It is natural for all of us to go through a fearful time following a tragedy. When our world has been torn apart, we worry about the stability of the larger world. We may find ourselves inappropriately concerned about our own safety and the safety of others. The same will hold true for our children. If the trauma is released and resolved in a healthy manner, these fears will subside as a stronger sense of personal power begins to surface. If the trauma is *not* released and remains *unresolved,* children may be prone to fearing their external world well into adulthood.

Unresolved trauma can lead to a variety of obsessive tendencies later in life. In most cases the common themes include *protect-yourself-from-them* behaviors. These behaviors may manifest in mild ways, such as constant verbal warnings about not trusting them, or in more extreme ways, like committing violent acts in an effort to harm or destroy *them.*

When young children do not feel safe they usually externalize their fear. One of the most common ways fear steps out of a child's unconscious and says, **Pay attention!** is by transforming itself into a monster during REM (rapid eye movement) sleep, or *dream-time.*

Occasionally, if the fears become overwhelming, the monster may gather the strength to straddle the dream-world, and suddenly become very real during the child's waking hours. If your child is having frightening experiences of this nature, you might consider seeking some guidance from a good child psychologist.

When children speak about their fear of monsters, do not belittle their fears or tell them "there is no such thing." Keep in mind the way children respond to puppets as if they were more real than the hand that holds them, and your task will become easier.

Think of the monster as being a puppet on the hand of fear. Speak to the *puppet,* and your children will eventually notice the *hand* on their own. If you tell them there is no such thing as a monster, you are denying them their very real fears. As a result, they will have no reason to believe you — or trust you.

Three Monster Tips:

1. When children report a monster sighting, respond to their concerns. Ask them to show you where it is. Quite often it will be in a pattern on the ceiling, in the wood grain on their door, or in the way the clothes are arranged in the closet. These kinds of monsters are easily chased away by rearranging the clothes in the closet, or (when monsters appear on the ceiling) by placing some artwork the child has created over them. In this way the monster vanishes beneath the child's personal power.

2. If your children still insist there is a monster in their room, tell the monster to *get out!* and if it ever comes back again you will spank it so hard it will pee its pants! This response usually gets the kids giggling, and at the same time creates a feeling of safety.

3. When monsters appear in dreams, encourage your children to draw pictures of the scary beasts in detail. After a drawing session with your children, look at the pictures and say, *"Let's ask the monster what it needs. What do you think it might say if we asked it that question? What do you think it will say the next time you ask it what it needs in your dream?"* These types of exercises help children regain their sense of personal power while addressing their fears face to face.

One of the other ways young children often deal with trauma is to externalize their fears onto other people. They begin to focus their anger and distrust on the people who are supposed to keep them safe such as parents, teachers, grandparents, police officers, and adult authority figures in general.

When this happens, the best solution is firm but *shameless* parenting. By shameless parenting I am referring to making *certain* our children realize we are disciplining them because they *did* something unfavorable, not because they *are* something unfavorable.

During times of crisis, children usually misbehave or *act out*. When their personal world suddenly changes shape, they will frantically search for the edges of their new (internal) environment. Animals placed in captivity will do the same thing. They will search the edges of their new container many times before settling into a routine.

Parents *are* the container for children in crisis. If you maintain the basic rules of your household, your children will soon lose their unruly behavior and settle into their own emotional healing. For example, if bedtime has always been 8:30, then make it a priority to maintain the same schedule during difficult times. When our children are free-falling they need a strong safety net. *We are the net. Be There!* Bending the rules will only create holes in the fabric, making the net unsafe.

Remember *shameless parenting* is vital to your children's healing process. When our baby girl died, I found my own parenting skills diminished dramatically. I became so overwhelmed and sleep-deprived that I was often short tempered with our son, Jason.

If I snapped at him, I tried to apologize immediately. I told him, "These *days I just seem to wake up feeling sad and angry. It is not your fault, and it has nothing to do with you. I would be this short-tempered even if nobody else were here with me."* I also promised him we would *both* sit down and relax for thirty seconds every time he told me I was getting too cranky. During one of these 30 second breathers a simple saying came to me: *Shape The Will - Nurture The Spirit.* I posted that saying in the kitchen and bath where I could see it often. I found that little reminder to be a constant aid in focusing my parenting skills.

Another *very* helpful thing we did was to honor the bedtime ritual without fail. No matter how exhausted or distracted we may have been, we all gathered together (*on time!*) to read a story or just share our thoughts at bedtime. Each time we did this it seemed as though the wounds of the day were healed. We also felt closer, and found we had fewer nightmares.

As mentioned in the section entitled *Turning The Tide,* studies have shown that children often do much better when they can have a new small pet of their own to nurture (like a kitten, or a small dog). If the child is under the age of six, the parent should handle the pet's feeding and training, and allow the child to enjoy just nurturing the animal.

Be tender in your discipline as your child develops new habits of feeding and grooming his or her pet. If your child is above the age of six (and mature enough to care for the animal) set up a large calendar listing the pet duties and have the youngster check them off daily.

Cooking together can be very therapeutic. The simple, soothing tasks of stirring and pouring can lead to natural conversation. It is one of the best ways I have found to get children to share their thoughts. I have used this technique with my own children as well as the children in my classroom. During the military involvement with Iraq, (several students had fathers who were involved) we scheduled one baking day a week. The children always looked forward to the soothing task of preparing food together. They also used the opportunity to talk over their fears about the war.

If the children are under the age of eight, you can fool them a little bit by stretching the amount of time needed to prepare the food. For example, from the time my son was three years old he talked freely about his joyful experiences and sulked silently about the upsetting ones. Whenever I detected a sulking attack, I would make a mental note to set aside a two hour cooking session. I couldn't always arrange to do it immediately, but within 24 hours of the sulking onset we were usually baking chocolate chip cookies together. (We arrived at this standby because it was the only recipe he would never refuse.) I would begin by pouring a little flour in his bowl, and then tell him it needed to be stirred for a good long time.

I kept this up with each ingredient until he began to open up. It wasn't until he was in high school that he discovered it takes about twelve minutes to prepare chocolate chip cookies from scratch! He was lovingly miffed with me when he discovered my tactics. Nevertheless,

I tried it again during a sulking attack when he was fifteen years old and discovered he was recovering from his first broken heart.

Now my grandson and I are enjoying the same tradition. His mother has *promised* me she won't let him know how long it actually takes to make ginger snaps (*his* favorite). If you want this system to work, keep in mind that you are not really stirring the batter. You are actually stirring up nurturing conversations.

When teens are hurting and pulling away, one great way to open communications is to get them into a car, *without headphones!* You might offer to buy them a new article of clothing, then insist on driving to a store that is having a sale several miles away. Car rides can be the beginning of wonderful conversations. I usually start by talking about my own life and then say something like, *I noticed you have been unusually quiet at the dinner table lately, did you notice that?* Another opening for communication I like to use is to describe any unusual behaviors such as *I noticed your hugs have been pretty limp lately, did you notice that?* or *It seems to me you were smiling much more last week than you have been this week. Is it my imagination, or have you been feeling a bit low these days?*

If after several of these attempts my kids still don't want to talk, I begin listing things I appreciate about them. Some examples might be how they behaved when we had company, how I respect this or that about them, etc. If they are hurting and are not ready to talk, thirty minutes of appreciation from one of their parents does a world of good anyway.

No matter what age your children may be, when they are upset and not sleeping enough insist on an early bedtime for at least four consecutive nights. Try to help them understand that this early bedtime schedule is not imposed upon them as a form of punishment, nor is it meant to be disrespectful of their physical maturity. It is simply a matter of respecting the basic needs of the human brain — at any age. Sleep deprivation will magnify our sorrows, fears, and doubts. Unfortunately, if left unchecked, it can alter the metabolism's balance and lead to a battle with severe depression.

> Come let us honor sleep,
> The sleep that knits up the
> raveled sleeve of care, the death
> of each day's life.
> Empty us of aches and pains,
> for we struggle as seeds through
> unyielding earth.
>
> – CONGREGATION OF ABRAXAS

If You Have Lost A Child

"You cannot now realize that you will ever feel better . . .
And yet this is a mistake. You are sure to be happy again."

–ABRAHAM LINCOLN

"In this sad world of ours,
sorrow comes to all.
It comes with the bitterest agony.
Perfect relief is not possible, except with
time. You cannot now realize that you
will ever feel better. . .
And yet this is a mistake. You are sure
to be happy again. To know this, which
is certainly true, will make you become
less miserable now.
I have experienced enough
to know what I say."

*Abraham Lincoln lost three sons: Edward, age 4; William, age 11; and Thomas, age 18. He comforted other bereaved parents with these words.

Our children are our children regardless of what their age may be. Losing an adult child can be as devastating as losing an infant. Mourning the loss of our children may be the most difficult task under the sun. The experience changes our lives forever.

In my own family, my husband, son and I each experienced a need for tender silence for several weeks after our baby girl died. We found that we had very few words during the initial phase of our healing. The details of her death would play over and over again in our minds. This happened both in our dreams and during waking hours.

Everyone seemed to be talking too fast. Perky people who tried to enliven us seemed particularly abrasive — even blasphemous. It was also very difficult for my husband and me to see other toddlers for a period of about two years. Please understand that we were sincerely delighted to see other parents enjoying their children. Yet, each time we saw these little ones an involuntary gulp of air just seemed to leap into our throats as our minds instantly replayed the scenes of our own daughter's death.

There is a ninety-eight percent divorce rate among families who experience child death. Our marriage is within the two percent that grew deeper. Our home is filled with love and laughter once again, and our family bond has strengthened immeasurably. While we each did many things to further our journey through the storm (grief counseling certainly being one of the most valuable) there were three prominent themes that seemed to help us most of all:

• The first was listening to our bodies over the rationalizations of our minds.

• The second was recognizing that unfathomable rage was part of the experience and if we denied it, misused it, or directed it at each other, we only gave it staying power.

• The third may be the most important and the most misunderstood. We discovered that what has been misnamed a natural "guilt process" for bereaved parents may be something much deeper— something more sacred, and something that has the possibility of connecting us to unknowable strength.

1. Listening to the body

When my mind said, *It is only 7:30 in the evening!* and my mouth said, *yawn,* I slept. When my mind said *it feels good to have these people here right now*, while my arms were clenching a pillow to my chest, I said, "Thank you so much for coming; I need to excuse myself and take a nap now."

When my mind said *I can't cry right now!* and my throat was swallowing a huge lump, I let the tears come. When this happened in public I played a mental game that proved to be quite helpful. Rather than trying to choke down the sorrow I imagined myself settling down to the bottom of the pain and purposefully sitting in the center of it.

When I did this my breathing expanded naturally, and a deep sense of relief came over me. I was repeatedly surprised at how seldom the tears emerged when I surrendered in this way. If tears did come, they would be the honest, eyes-opened kind of tears; the kind that seem to speak to the humanity in all of us, rather than the kind that seem to repel or embarrass others.

2. Letting the rage wash through

Rage can disguise itself as "other people's" shortcomings with surprising credibility! It begins by making other people seem annoying, then progresses to making them seem somewhat incompetent. Finally, they become intolerable idiots who must be reckoned with!

I tried to imagine frustrating "problems" with the incompetent people around me as being *caution signs* along the roadway to an angry outburst. As the number of road signs increased, I knew that I was on a one-way road to rage and, willing or unwilling, I was going to have to hang on and take that dreadful ride.

If these overpowering feelings suddenly consumed me in public, I would excuse myself to the rest room, close myself in a stall and just try to get as angry as I possibly could without making much noise. If I needed to make noise, I would flush the toilet. My misdirected anger decreased dramatically once I began following the impulse (finding a secluded place to release my frustration in short but intense spurts) rather than stifling it.

Since my family members were on the same road to rage, angry outbursts happened at home much more often. We made a pact that when one of us became reckless with blame, the others would just keep saying *Remember I love you.*

In your own life, don't hurt the other vulnerable members of your family with angry words! Let the rage rumble through you, but don't allow it to become blame. When the family is in such a fragile state, it may just break apart completely (and most do)! Be Careful!

Compassionate Friends is an organization of bereaved parents centered in the United States. Their services include support groups, counseling available by phone, family activities and a monthly newsletter. We found their support invaluable. If you cannot find a chapter in your area, consider locating the nearest membership center and make a connection by phone.

3. The sacred place

When our children die or are harmed in any way, the terrible details tumble over and over in our minds. We replay the scene with ten thousand *what ifs* and *if onlys* scattered throughout. Most books on the subject of parental grief name this phenomenon as a natural "guilt process"—a passing state of grief.

I think this assumption is an attempt to logically interpret a primal response that goes much deeper than cognitive thinking. Removing the *guilt process* label allows us to reach past logical misinterpretations and enter into levels of our humanity which are much more substantial, and certainly more sacred.

Within each of us are silent convictions that run deeper than words, deeper than thoughts; movements that stir from the soul in an *instant* without any consent from the conscious mind.

These unspoken convictions can leap forth enabling us to lift up a car to free a child, risk our own lives to save a friend from danger, or sacrifice our own bodies for the sake of our young. When we are unable to protect our children from danger, I believe this unwavering impulse to leap to their aid continues.

My husband's and my experience was not unlike that of most bereaved parents. Our desire to leap to our daughter's aid continued long after her death. Eventually, we found that respecting this feeling as a repeated primal urge to protect our young brought us to an ever-deepening sense of peace. Because this process involves embracing feelings which go beyond words, we call it the *sacred embrace* process. Here is how it works:

When the tragic scenes replay in your mind, don't attach words to your thoughts. If words come in, try replacing them with a song. Don't cower from the internal images and feelings, allow them to flow through; just don't make the mistake of misnaming the experience. Think of it as that "leap of love" you were deprived of, and *leap as you would have anyway!* Not from a place of regret or apology, just free-fall into your love for your child, and grieve from that place of purity.

We have suggested this process to other bereaved parents, and to family members who felt they carried some responsibility for the death of a loved one. In each case, the families who used the *sacred embrace* process found it brought them to the source of their feelings. In contrast to the more traditional approach of attempting to fit these primal feelings into words (like guilt or shame) they also found the sacred embrace process allowed them a more direct route to emotional release.

When the scenes of my daughter's death would replay in my mind, if I could keep my thoughts wordless, I would have an experience of just falling through my love for her. This happened repeatedly until I reached a depth of love I had not known before. At that point (a few months later) the falling feeling changed into a sensation of a calm fullness. This sensation is very difficult to describe. It might be better articulated in a letter I wrote to my daughter, Laney, on the anniversary of her death. A small section of this letter is included in the Author's Note, but I would like to share it with other bereaved families in its entirety.

My son, Jason, and I benefited from burying our letters at Laney's grave site. If you have surviving siblings, Jason's letter may encourage them to write one of their own. His letter follows mine on a separate page, so you can share it with your children. (You will find both letters in the following chapter.)

Angel, Good-bye
(my letter to my daughter)

"In the depth of winter, I finally learned
that within me there lay an invincible summer."

— ALBERT CAMUS

My dear Laney, I would have fought anyone or anything for you. I would have shown my claws, flashed my teeth, and fought beyond my last breath for you. But I watched as death came in utter stillness, uncurled our deep embrace and took you from me. I was holding on as tightly as I possibly could without crushing you.

There was no place to throw myself to save you — no spaces between us I could fit into. And while I respected your choice to go, I had no ability to tame the wild anguish that just kept leaping further and further forth to find you as you were going. My screaming came from the primal place where the mothers of all species dwell. A place untouched by thought.

A place that fuels a mother's leaping with *fire!* Like quick claws of lightning leaping down from the sky. Searing past time. Leaping past thought, snapping the predator's bones beneath her feet. . . .But when the predator strikes from afar, the mother's leaping arches across the darkness and falls through the endless night, alone.

For what seemed like a long time I feared the crying would never stop assaulting me. Yet I believed that if I could stay with the grief, I could one day begin to heal this relentless anguish. While I still miss you *terribly* the healing must have eased in unnoticed, as I am now realizing the gift you gave me with your death as well as with your life. Thank you for teaching me to love with all my being while losing the one I am loving. Thank you for giving me my worst fear so I could live through it knowing if I can do this, I can do anything. Thank you for the amazing experience of a depth of prayer I had not believed possible, and for the realization that I cannot pray for God's will and then accept it selectively.

Thank you for teaching me to cry without hiding, to let the tears come when they come, to cry with my head up, my chest full, and to no longer apologize for sorrow.

Now, when I catch myself cowering at life, if I close my eyes and remember your face, I find the courage to be awkward and vulnerable once again. It seems that a willingness to settle into this awkwardness and vulnerability is the only focus needed to remain loving in almost any situation. This may prove to be the finest gift you have given me.

This simple willingness usually takes all the courage I can muster, no matter how often I practice it. When I am successful, the thoughts which generally limit my life temporarily lose their strength. They no longer have my full attention. My attention turns to the person I am listening to, the thing I am watching, the way the wind smells, the task at hand. Thank you my precious daughter, I will always love you deeply with all my soul.

I have thundered the path
of my predator enraged. . .
churned the underworld snarling
and wild, paced the floor weeping
with my own dying child.

These lives and I,
this death and I, are beginning
to recognize one another.
I am a mud maiden stirred from
the earth, dancing all distances near.
Moist supple bones pulsing new blood.

Dry powdered bones carried
on the wind.
Dying ashes flickering in the breeze.

I am the living flame
of my own dream. . . All faces,
my face. All breathing, my breath.

The young bird falling, falling,
falling, then remembering
its wings.

—ALISON ASHER excerpt from, *My Walk on this Earth*

Jason's Letter:

Dear Laney,

I love you very much and I wish that we could be together. I have been missing you a lot, mostly at night.

We know it was God's choice to take you back, but we don't know why. We are very glad God kept mom alive.

We all love you very much. We have been having a pretty hard time, but it doesn't stop us from having fun sometimes. I hope you are having fun too.

We all love you very much. It feels good to just keep saying that over and over again. That's why I tell you that so many times.

I still have some crying left inside, but it won't come out yet. Crying about you got lots of my anger out. We all have been crying quite a lot.

We pray for you every day.

Sometimes I light your candle and say the prayer all by myself.

Today we are going to plant a tree, and it will just be your tree forever.

I love you.

Your big brother,

Jason

Goodnight God . . .
I like the world
very much.
I'm glad you made
the plants and trees
survive with the rain
and summers . . .
I like how God feels
around everyone in the world.
God, I am very happy that
I live on you.
Your arms
clasp around the world.
I like you
and your friends . . .
I hope you have
a good time
being the world.

— DANU BAXTER,
four and a half years old

Additional Research

"The whole of science is nothing more than a refinement of everyday thinking." –ALBERT EINSTEIN

Throughout my twenty years of experience teaching children with physical and emotional challenges, I have used stories and parables as a means of educating the children and their parents. It seems that people of all ages tend to retain pertinent information when it is related in story form. Recent studies on memory function support this assertion. Currently, scientists are discovering how memories are recorded and retrieved from the human brain.

The hippocampus, which is located in the *limbic system*, greatly influences the function of memory. When the limbic system becomes emotionally overwhelmed, it can close the gateways to the logical levels of the brain. This process can make rote memories almost entirely inaccessible during emotionally stressful situations. In other words, the brain's gateway to memorized information is usually closed when one is very upset.

This is why people often find themselves acting out old patterns of behavior during emotional experiences while newly memorized responses fail to surface until the overwhelming emotions subside.

Therefore, if one learns new ways to deal with these emotions by rote, it may seem impossible to retrieve that information when it is needed most. Yet, if this same information is learned in *story form*, these new concepts tend to sink into the memory at a deeper level and can be much easier to recall when needed most, during stressful times.

I have written the *Soaring Into The Storm* parable based upon these findings and with the intention of reaching the reader's deeper memory. Long after the book has been closed I hope important images from the story will resurface and offer some gentle guidance through future emotional storms.

The cultures with the highest rate of social pressure to repress sorrow tend to be the same cultures with higher rates of violence, alcoholism, depression, and suicide. Could it be that these tendencies are interrelated? Recent medical investigation has found that crying causes a beneficial chemical change in the body which helps to stabilize strong emotions. The suppression of the urge to cry forces the body to eliminate the chemical imbalance in ways which may be detrimental not only to the individual, but to society as a whole. Psychiatrist, Dr. N. Rashidi of Kings Park Hospital in New York, makes a strong argument for changing our cultural response to sorrow in the following medical study:

The Psychodynamics of Crying

"If people were culturally allowed to cry, encouraged to release their tensions, and acknowledge their inherent human weaknesses, there would be less necessity for fighting, violence, and war, and a calmer state of mind would prevail. There would be a decrease in the incidence of emotional problems, suicidal deaths, peptic ulcers, and probably other psychosomatic diseases. The study and analysis of crying in psychiatry reveals a wealth of information about one's unconscious and early childhood experiences. This is particularly important, as, unlike the interpretation of dreams, crying can be studied on an on-going experimental and research basis."[1]

> The cultures with the highest rate of social pressure to repress sorrow tend to be the same cultures with higher rates of violence, alcoholism, depression, and suicide. Could it be that these tendencies are interrelated? Scientists & psychologists agree that this could indeed be the case.

Psychotherapists Peg Mayo and Dr. David Feinstein co-authored a marvelous book entitled *Rituals for Living and Dying*. This work includes processes for healing from trauma and loss, personal and professional insights, and a number of case histories. The following quotes point directly to the mental and physical dynamics of unexpressed emotional pain:

From the book *Rituals for Living and Dying*

"It is clear that the body and mind interact intimately. Many a peptic ulcer has been traced to an agitated mind. Containing grief carries a fearful danger of physical and emotional sickness. We do literally have wounds from our sufferings — the broken heart we feel in our chest is the real, beating organ that pumps our blood.

Unrelieved sorrow has led many to seek solace in alcohol and drugs or to retreat into the living death of mental withdrawal... emptying out is part of the growth necessary to transmute grief to creativity. To contain, deny, or repress our pain may lead to personality-distorting depression.

As a therapist, I'm on the alert when a bereaved client doesn't weep. The swollen eyes, runny nose, and gasping breath of hard crying vividly show the energy involved...

To contain our wails and complaints, we use great amounts of energy, energy that is then unavailable for creative living. We must discharge what is hurtful. We will make space for other emotions and free the energies that had been devoted to containing the pain. When we are effective in discharge, we unburden our psyche of graceless misery rather than holding it inside like a growing canker."[2]

Scientists are drawing the conclusion that people who are able to cry may enjoy better physical, emotional, and mental health. They may also have more success in personal relationships and find it easier to simply enjoy life.

> The question is, are people
> who feel crying is a weakness
> stronger in character
> or weaker at heart?. . .
> Have they truly developed the
> ability to
> contain their tears,
> or have they simply become
> adept at avoiding
> emotional situations and
> authentic relationships?

Not surprisingly, people who find it difficult to reach past emotional barriers also tend to have difficulties in personal relationships. The question is, are people who feel crying is a weakness stronger in character or weaker at heart? How can one embrace the joys of life while habitually stifling important information the body is trying to communicate to the brain?

Medical & Psychological Research Agrees

Randolph R. Cornelius, an associate professor of psychology at Vassar College, explains that tears originate in the parasympathetic nervous system and are produced in response to *fight-or-flight syndrome* – which is triggered by stress. The *fight-or-flight* response is designed to keep the body alive under extreme adverse conditions, such as a life-threatening physical assault.

Unfortunately, the brain often misinterprets extremely stressful situations (such as a divorce or the loss of a job) as being life-threatening and continually prepares the body to fight or flee. When this condition is sustained, stress-induced toxins begin to accumulate, causing a precarious imbalance within the system. Tears have been chemically proven to remove these toxins and to help restore the body's natural balance.[3]

A number of medical scientists and psychologists comment on their similar findings in the following unrelated studies:[4] Dr. William Frey, biochemist and director of the Ramsey Dry Eye and Tear Research Center in Minneapolis explains that emotional crying is an excretory function. The tears we shed when we're upset are high in protein. Tears also contain hormones—ACTH and Prolactin, for example—that are present during stress; thus, weeping may be a way for the body to rid itself of these stress-induced substances.[5]

According to Dr. Frey, the reason people usually feel better after crying is that they may be removing, in their tears, the chemicals that build up during emotional stress. His research indicates that tears rid the body of various toxins and other wastes.

Alan Wolfelt, Ph.D., and a professor at the University of Colorado Medical School, works primarily with people who are mourning the death of a loved one. 'In my clinical experience with thousands of mourners, I have consistently observed changes in the physical [appearance] following the expression of tears... not only do people feel better after crying; they also look better.'[6]

> Tears actually remove stress-induced toxic chemicals from the body. They also contain beta-endorphin, one of the body's natural pain relievers.

As far back as 1957 it was discovered that emotional tears are chemically different from tears that result because of an eye irritation. Emotional tears contain more protein and beta-endorphin, one of the body's natural pain relievers. Margaret Crepeau, Ph.D., and a professor of nursing at Marquette University, has studied the subject of tears from both physical and emotional angles. She claims that healthy people view tears positively, while people plagued with various illnesses see them as unnecessary and even humiliating. Dr. Crepeau states: "I found that well men and women cried more tears more often and at more times than did men and women with ulcers and colitis."[7]

Consequently, in the school of nursing at Marquette University, nurses as well as those in training are urged not to automatically provide tranquilizers to weeping patients, but to allow the tears to do their own therapeutic work. Dr. Crepeau states, "Laughter and tears are two inherent natural medicines whereby we can reduce duress, let out negative feelings, and recharge. They truly are the body's own best resources."[8]

What if you can't cry?

Since research is giving credence to the idea that good health is connected to the shedding of tears, those who are unable to cry should look more closely to see if they are unconsciously blocking the flow of tears. For some people this may mean therapy. One woman, normally a non-crier, who grew up in a family in which keeping a stiff upper lip was the rule, found herself crying deeply almost every time she met with her therapist. She says, "There were latent feelings all bottled up inside of me for years. After every teary session I felt better and better."

Should tears be controlled?

The simple answer is no. Very few people overreact and cry for the wrong reasons. The fact is, most people would do better to let go and have a good cry periodically. Experts agree that it is unwise to make a habit of holding back tears.

> Dr. Margaret Crepeau, professor of nursing at Marquette University, has studied the subject of tears from both physical and emotional angles. She claims that healthy people view tears positively, while people plagued with various illnesses see them as unnecessary and even humiliating.

A word of caution, however, for those who cry every time they're criticized, have a fight with a friend, or experience normal work frustrations. One therapist says, "People who cry easily should feel glad they're able to be in touch with their feelings. But if they are crying a lot in response to criticism, they should try to get some help. That kind of crying is an alarm bell that warns of some deep hurt or loss of self-esteem that is triggered whenever anyone says anything negative." Perhaps the best advice about tears comes from Charles Dickens, who declares in Oliver Twist that crying "...opens the lungs, washes the countenance, exercises the eyes, and softens down the temper. So cry away!"[9]

In her letter to the author, Dr. Judith A. Peters (Ph.D., Neurophysiology) offered her professional insights on emotional repression, memory formation, and the significance of teaching new concepts through story-telling:

"The emotional determinants of cognition are largely overlooked in our culture. [Most school systems tend to] rely heavily on rote learning. Rote learning is generally non-experiential, lacks emotional tone, and thus bypasses important neuro-emotional connections within the psyche or 'subconscious mind.'

"While research struggles to determine the precise anatomic structures within the limbic and reticular areas of the brain that house these mind-body states, educators, therapists, and all of us must begin to apply what we already know. The way emotions color the learning process affects not only the application but also the appropriate retrieval of learning. To short-circuit the learning process by denying the emotional components involved is to shift the fragile neuronal plasticity of the brain toward dysfunction. This dysfunctional neural circuitry inhibits the natural joy for living and learning that we all innately possess. I think this important issue is elegantly addressed in *Soaring Into The Storm* with the beautiful analogies that unfold during the story."[10]

> The emotional
> determinants of cognition
> are largely overlooked
> in our culture. . .
> The way emotions color
> the learning process
> affects not only the application
> but also the appropriate
> retrieval of learning. . .
>
> – Dr. Judith A. Peters

Findings Specific to Young Children

This section focuses on helping young children heal from emotional traumas (divorce, death, loss of a home, a difficult move, or loss of a beloved pet) and examines some possible sources of violent tendencies in our youth.

Contributors to this section are as follows: Dr. Joyce Brothers, an award-winning author and psychologist specializing in family issues; Dr. Ronald G. Slaby, Senior Scientist at the Education Development Center in Newton, Massachusetts and Lecturer at Harvard, and his associate Wendy Conklin Roedell, who co-authored *Psychological Development In The Early Years* for the New York Academic Press. Dr. Brothers contributed the following specifically for *Soaring Into The Storm*:

Children and Loss by Dr. Joyce Brothers

"Usually, by the time we're adults, we have some first-hand experience with this grim presence that casts such a cloud over our spirits. Although we may become familiar with loss and grief, we never become immune to the emptiness, the anger, and hurt that so often accompany the sickness and death of a friend or loved one. Children, however, are frequently overwhelmed by the flood of emotions that rage within them, and one of the most common results is that they strike out at those they love most, or act in ways that, to adults, may seem totally inappropriate. They may, in their sorrow, alienate friends and family. As author, Alison Asher, points out, as they turn their anger toward their friends, they may perceive the world to be angry and against them.

"Unfortunately, all too often, adults, in an attempt to shelter children from pain, shut them out through silence. When this happens, children invent their own explanations for what is taking place, their imagination runs wild, and the reality becomes even more frightening, and more terrifying. Losses need to be explained, honored and respected, whether the loss involves a family pet, a friend who is moving to another community, or a friend or family member who's lost in illness, or death. Obviously, how illness and death are explained must depend, in part, upon the child's age.

"Children under five, for example, may not see death as permanent, and may assume the dead will return at some later date. Generally speaking, the more honest a parent can be, the better for the child; for things that are left cloudy or unspoken may come back to haunt the future. Children need to be told by adults that they're not in any way responsible for the loss, or the sadness that has struck them and their family. Although it is sometimes difficult for adults to understand, little children are prone to the kind of magical thinking that may lead them to worry because of a careless remark they may have made about the afflicted person, or a dark thought that passed through their mind when they were angry at that person. They need to be reassured of their innocence and of the love that the ill or dying person holds for them. If possible, they need time to prepare for what's going to happen, and if the person is dying, they need to be able to express their own deep feelings toward the loved one.

> Unfortunately. . .
> adults, in an attempt
> to shelter children from pain,
> shut them out through silence.
> When this happens, children invent
> their own explanations
> for what is taking place,
> their imagination runs wild
> and the reality becomes even more
> frightening. . .
>
> — DR. JOYCE BROTHERS

"When these farewells are not possible, the child needs to be able to express these feelings of love and grief to those adults who survive, and who, even though they are also in pain, are able to listen to these small voices. Children may deny loss because they've been taught to be afraid of tears. If little boys are taught that it's unmanly to cry, they will have an especially difficult time, not only as children, but as adults. Adults sometimes forget that youngsters don't automatically empathize and project themselves into the minds and souls of others. They need to be taught that we are all linked; the bond is love and a willingness to share."[11]

Dr. Brothers Expresses Her Concerns About Children and Violence

"In some ways, I often wonder if perhaps today's children may not have a more difficult task learning to empathize than did children in the past, not only because our world is more violent, but because that violence is brought into the home by television. It seems, and often *is*, unreal. The line between make-believe pain and loss and real pain and loss must, at times, seem puzzling and complex. If the pain is only make-believe, part of a play on TV, then we quickly learn how not to identify, how to withhold our tears and our feelings, but I worry that this withholding, this "cool" attitude toward suffering can become a pattern of denial and withdrawal. Communication between parent and child can be the key in restoring sensitivity and compassion. Until we are able to respect ourselves, even in our grief, our anger, and our sadness, it will be difficult to respect the pain we see in others."[12]

The way we guide our children through emotional turmoil helps determine their ability (or inability) to empathize. Their ability to feel compassion toward themselves and others seems to be directly proportionate to the level of violence they will allow in their lives. This observation seems to hold true whether the violence is coming *from* them or *to* them. Dr. Slaby, Senior Scientist at the Education Development Center in Newton, Massachusetts, agrees that bonding combined with open communications between parent and child can be vital in curbing violent tendencies in youth.

Dr. Slaby's Findings

"Violence does not simply appear mysteriously and full blown in an adolescent. Rather, violent patterns of behavior — or alternatively, nonviolent, socially constructive patterns of behavior — are acquired by children through specific and alterable processes of socialization and development. Thus, a key to preventing the development of violence-supporting patterns of behavior lies in early, systematic, and continual intervention that reduces those social experiences that contribute to violence and builds those internal resources that protect children against violence..."[13] For purposes of this review, we will simply use the term *aggression* to refer to those actions that involve actual or intended physical or psychological injury to another individual.

"...In an exemplary longitudinal study, Eron et al., examined aggressive behaviors in eight-year-olds. Ten years later, when they were eighteen, aggression was again assessed.

"One childhood factor that was predictive of aggression in young adults was the children's degree of identification with their parents, as indicated by the similarities between the parents' and the child's independent ratings of their own style of expressing common behavior (e.g. walking fast or slow, talking fast or slow). Children who were closely identified with their parents at the age of eight tended to be less aggressive ten years later..."[14]

The findings from the ten noted medical professionals, psychologists, and scientists quoted in this chapter speak to dramatically altering our cultural perspective on emotional expression. Additionally, as Dr. Joyce Brothers and Dr. Slaby point out, the parent/child bond is vital to the development of nonviolent behaviors in our youth. *"Children who were closely identified with their parents at the age of eight tended to be less aggressive ten years later..."*[15] *"They [children] need to be taught that we are all linked..."*[16] It seems that our ability to identify with one another begins within the family. Our ability to overcome adversity determines the level of compassion that comes both *from* us, and *to* us; and our ability to care for one another determines the quality of our humanity.

A Request From The Author

I am currently collecting letters from people who have triumphed over adversity for the companion book entitled *Soaring Letters*. I am particularly interested in the main questions posed in the beginning of this book: *Why do some people become hard-hearted following an emotional ordeal while others seem to emerge from even greater difficulty with a deeper capacity to enjoy life? How do I nurture these qualities in myself? How do I teach these valuable life-skills to my children?*

Additionally, readers would like to know, *Was there a specific turning point during your ordeal? Who were the personal heroes in your life (the people who significantly influenced your life in a short span of time), and how did they inspire you?*

If someone you know has a glorious smile, loving nature, and a strong measure of wisdom, please encourage him or her to write me. They must write *Soaring Letters* on the envelope, or their letter will be forwarded to the wrong department. If the people you are encouraging to contact me feel shy about doing so, consider interviewing them yourself. (Your letters, videos, and audio tapes will not be returned, so make a copy!) Please understand that I will not respond to you individually. The purpose is not to speak to me personally, but to bring warmth, light, and promise to others.

Additional Research Section Endnotes

[1] *The Psychodynamics of Crying*, Dr. N. Rashidi, Psychiatric Unit, Kings Park Hospital, Kings Park, New York, CMDIA Medical Dialogue, pp. 40/1— 66/67

[2] *Rituals for Living and Dying*, Feinstein/Mayo, pp. 128-145

[3] Quote: Randolph R. Cornelius, Associate professor of psychology, Vassar College, Poughkeepsie, New York

[4] Article excerpted from Victor Parachin, Vibrant Life Magazine v8 n6 p4(2)

[5] Quote: Dr. William H. Frey, Biochemist and Director of the Ramsey Dry Eye and Tear Research Center, Saint Paul, Minnesota

[6] Quote: Alan Wolfelt, Ph.D. and Professor, University of Colorado Medical School, Boulder, Colorado

[7 & 8] Quote: Margaret Crepeau, Ph.D. and professor of nursing at Marquette University

[9] End of excerpt from by Victor Parachin, Vibrant Life, Magazine v8 n6 p4(2)

[10] Quote: Dr. Judith A. Peters, Neurophysiologist

[11 & 12] Dr. Joyce Brother's, Submission to the author

[13] Dr. Ronald G. Slaby, statement to the press concerning the Report of the American Psychological Association Commission on Violence and Youth

[14] Dr. Ronald G. Slaby and Wendy Conklin Roedell *Psychological Development In The Early Years*, New York Academic Press, pp. 97-149

[15] Excerpted from Dr. Ron Slaby and Wendy Conkilin Rodell *Psychological Development In The Early Years*

[16] Excerpted from Dr. Joyce Brother's submission

If there is a light
in the soul,
there will be beauty
in the person.

If there is beauty
in the person,
there will be harmony
in the house.

If there is harmony
in the house,
there will be order
in the nation.

If there is order
in the nation,
there will be peace
in the world.

— LAO TZU, Ancient Chinese Philosopher

ABOUT THE SWANS

For thousands of years swans have been portrayed as a symbols of transformation in folklore, legends and myths. As their migratory patterns stirred the skies between the continents, inspiration seemed to stir the in hearts of storytellers around the globe. The Native Americans have a long-standing myth about a young bride who transforms into a red swan in an effort to save her beloved from danger. Ancient New Zealand folklore teaches that the Maori were descendants of the beautiful black swans which are native to that area. They tell a tale of a great flood that drove their people to the mountain peaks. As the water finally consumed the land, the Maori transformed into a great flock of wild swans and flew to safety.

In keeping with the universal human response to these majestic creatures, the European culture has revered swans for centuries portraying their mystery and beauty in a variety of art forms including painting, sculpture, dance, costume, and verse. Perhaps the most renowned of the European swan stories is the tale of the ugly duckling, a downtrodden outcast who transforms into a respected leader among his peers.

Why have human beings revered these magnificent animals since the dawning of time? Could it be that their steady nurturing behavior reminds us of our own higher nature? Swans are steadfastly monogamous. Their family bond is unshakable involving both parents in the feeding, guidance and fierce protection of the young. During migratory flights the stronger birds fly in front of the weaker members of the flock, allowing them to be carried along by the updraft.

Their lengthy courtship is gracefully expressed through a magnificent dance. Certain species actually form the familiar valentine outline with their necks as part of their courtship ritual. Some sociologists speculate that the heart shaped symbol for love may have come from this elegant dance. Although each couple bonds for life, the male courts the female anew every year, tenderly inviting her to dance with him prior to their intimate interchange. In many cases the bond becomes so indelible that when one swan meets with an untimely death, its mate may grieve so deeply that it too dies within a few weeks.

The main characters of the *Soaring Into The Storm* parable are trumpeter swans: glorious creatures with wing spans of up to nine feet. The trumpeter's wingspan, body weight, and long, thick neck combine to make it the world's largest migratory bird. In the early 1800's one North American naturalist recalled *"the deafening sound of feathers"* lifting these giants to the sky by the thousands (a deafening sound my imagination often welcomes!) By the mid 1900's, however, the trumpeters had nearly vanished from the earth. Their soft underbellies had been used as powder puffs by thousands of European women, and their huge wing feathers had been harvested for use as quill pens and shipped across the globe.

With the help of the human hands that had once nearly destroyed the trumpeter, these glorious birds are beginning to return to the wild. As a direct result of our experience creating this book, my husband and I have become a part of this project. We have created a wildlife refuge by reconditioning an old irrigation reservoir where we are raising and releasing trumpeter swans.

After enjoying a fair amount of time in their inspiring yet formidable presence, one begins to wonder who is raising whom. We are learning a great deal about our own inner nature and our relationship as husband and wife through observing their behavior. Not surprisingly, we are in the process of building an addition to our home for the sole purpose of enjoying the elegant communion of nonverbal expression through dance.

"Papa and Gramma" a portrait of the author and her husband
by Samuel Parker

ABOUT THE AUTHOR

Alison Asher is a shamelessly proud mother and grandmother who would have happily included pictures of her children and grandchildren in this publication had the editor given his consent. She brings to this book more than twenty years of teaching experience working with physically and emotionally challenged youth and children with unusual learning styles. She and her husband, Leonard Krause, (who speaks eight languages and acts as her interpreter) have served on a number of international delegations and have conducted interviews for this book in the United States, Canada, Cuba, South Africa, the United Kingdom, Turkey, Spain, Portugal, Indonesia, Thailand, Japan, Hong Kong, Tibet, and the People's Republic of China.

Nationally recognized as an educational consultant and a seminar leader on topics such as innovative teaching techniques, parenting, family unity, and emotional healing, Ms. Asher offers her professional insights combined with her experience of recovery from many personal tragedies including the death of her youngest child. She owes her artistic abilities to her older sister Toni, and her delightful storytelling abilities to her younger sister Christine, whose ". . .sparkling eyes eagerly insisted on an *original* bedtime story nightly."

ACKNOWLEDGMENTS

I would especially like to thank the many families around the globe who welcomed my husband and me into their lives as we gathered research for this series. Thank you for answering difficult questions honestly, speaking of painful memories openly, and sometimes weeping deeply. It was in your keeping that Young Swan learned how the rivers feel when their edges thin as they taste the saltwater — and all their disguises dissolve as they become one ocean.

It seems appropriate to me that we have brought *Soaring Into The Storm* to life in a family spirit, as we are presently working to create *a Family* category in the Library of Congress for books such as these. Books that cross age barriers and are designed for the family to share can be difficult to market. Simply finding an appropriate place for them in bookstores can be a challenge because at this point in time a family section does not exist. The shelf-space in book stores and libraries is segregated by age: child, juvenile, young adult, and adult.

Presently, you will find books for adults *concerning* the family, and stories for children *about* family issues. This, however, is one of the first books designed specifically *for* the family — beginning with a fictional story for children and adults alike, followed by a nonfiction self-help section focused on all family members, and published in larger print for the grandparents. *Soaring Into The Storm* is breaking new ground in these areas on three continents.

I would like to extend a *special* note of appreciation to the wonderful people who previewed the manuscript. Because so many of you took the time to submit your support in writing, *Soaring* was able to gain the respect needed to find its way to Dr. Joyce Brothers and Jacqueline Kennedy Onassis — both of whom I appreciate deeply.

Ms. Kennedy Onassis received the manuscript during the latter stages of her illness. At a point in her life when each day must have been very precious, she took the time to read the book cover to cover. She then mailed my agent one of the only letters of encouragement she ever sent an author and signed it in her own hand. This unexpected act of grace and kindness stunned me at the time, and still inspires some occasional teardrops. Each time I pass her letter (framed above my desk), I wonder if I would have been as gracious under similar circumstances.

Dr. N. Rashidi excerpt from, *The Psychodynamics of Crying*, Psychiatric Unit, Kings Park Hospital., Kings Park, N.Y., USA. Dr. N. Rashidi, CMDIA Medical Dialogue.

Dr. David Feinstein & Peg Elliott Mayo excerpt from *Rituals for Living and Dying,* Copyright by Peg Elliott Mayo and David Feinstein. Reprinted by permission of Harper San Francisco, a division of HarperCollins Publishers.

Dr. Alan Wolfelt, Dr. Margaret Crepeau and Dr. William H. Frey, excerpts appeared in an article entitled *Fears about tears? Why crying is good for you!* Copyright by Victor Parachin, *Vibrant Life Magazine* v8 n6 p4(2). Reprinted by permission of the author.

Dr. Ronald G. Slaby excerpts from his statement to the press concerning the *Report of the American Psychological Association Commission on Violence and Youth.* Additional excerpts from, *Psychological Development In The Early Years,* New York Academic Press by Dr. Ronald G. Slaby & Wendy Conklin Roedell. Reprinted by permission of Dr. Slaby.

John Daniel excerpt from his poem *Of Earth* from the book *Common Ground, Poems by John Daniel* Copyright 1988 by John Daniel. Reprinted by permission of Confluence Press, Inc.

Gretel Ehrlich excerpt from *Islands, The Universe, Home* by Gretel Ehrlich Copyright 1991 by Gretel Ehrlich. Reprinted by permission of Viking Penguin, a division of Penguin Books USA Inc.

Bill Moyers excerpt from, *Healing And The Mind* by Bill Moyers. Copyright 1993 by Bill Moyers. Reprinted by permission of Doubleday, a division of Bantam, Doubleday, Dell Publishing Group.

Kahlil Gibran excerpt from *Jesus the Son of Man* by Kahlil Gibran. Copyright 1928 Reprinted by permission of Alfred A Knopf, a division of Random House.

Congregation of Abraxas excerpts from, *The book of Hours.* Copyright 1985 by Congregation of Abraxas Reprinted by permission of Mr. Harry Thor, Congregation of Abraxas Scribe.

All other quotes were either submitted to Ms. Asher directly in the form of a letter for use in this book, or are believed to be public domain.

A sincere effort has been made to locate all rights holders and to clear reprint permissions. If any required acknowledgments have been omitted, or any rights overlooked, it is unintentional and forgiveness is requested. If notified the publisher will be pleased to rectify any omission in future editions.